Man and the Renaissance

MAN AND THE RENAISSANCE

ANDREW MARTINDALE

Senior Lecturer in the School of Fine Arts,
University of East Anglia

McGRAW-HILL BOOK COMPANY
NEW YORK · TORONTO

General Editors

BERNARD S. MYERS   TREWIN COPPLESTONE
New York   *London*

PREHISTORIC AND PRIMITIVE MAN
Dr Andreas Lommel, Director of the Museum of Eth-
nology, Munich

THE ANCIENT WORLD
Professor Giovanni Garbini, Institute of Near Eastern
Studies, University of Rome

THE CLASSICAL WORLD
Dr Donald Strong, Assistant Keeper, Department of
Greek and Roman Antiquities, British Museum, London

THE EARLY CHRISTIAN AND BYZANTINE WORLD
Professor Jean Lassus, Institute of Art and Archaeology,
University of Paris

THE WORLD OF ISLAM
Dr Ernst J. Grube, Associate Curator in Charge, Islamic
Department, Metropolitan Museum of Art, New York

THE ORIENTAL WORLD
Jeannine Auboyer, Keeper at the Musée Guimet, Paris
Dr Roger Goepper, Director of the Museum of Far Eastern
Art, Cologne

THE MEDIEVAL WORLD
Peter Kidson, Conway Librarian, Courtauld Institute of
Art, London

MAN AND THE RENAISSANCE
Andrew Martindale, Senior Lecturer in the School of
Fine Arts, University of East Anglia

THE AGE OF BAROQUE
Michael Kitson, Lecturer in the History of Art, Courtauld
Institute of Art, London

THE MODERN WORLD
Norbert Lynton, Head of the School of Art History and
General Studies, Chelsea School of Art, London

Library of Congress Catalog Card Number 66-15837
40650
© PAUL HAMLYN LIMITED 1966

PRINTED IN THE NETHERLANDS BY JOH. ENSCHEDÉ EN ZONEN
GRAFISCHE INRICHTING N.V.   HAARLEM

*Previous pages: Monument to Erasmo da Narni, called
'the Gattamelata', by Donatello. Padua*

List of Contents

Colour Plates

Italy during the Renaissance
Heavy line indicates limits of the Papal States

Towards a New Style

1. **Benozzo Gozzoli.** *The Journey of the Magi.* 1459. Fresco. Chapel, Palazzo Medici-Riccardi, Florence. In spite of its ostensible religious subject, this work probably gives a fair idea of a 15th-century state procession, with members of the local court taking part. Evidence of 'conspicuous expenditure' on clothes and horse-trappings is abundant, for the 'state' of a medieval or Renaissance prince was demonstrated visibly by the number and quality of his attendants.

Since the decline of the Roman Empire, the inhabitants of Italy have had to suffer many foreigners, either as members of marauding armies, or as pilgrims and 'tourists' avaricious for treasures which Italy possessed and the northern nations did not. Moreover, Italians have always stressed the differences which separated them from 'barbarians beyond the Alps'. This feeling is clearly apparent in the writing of Petrarch and Dante; in 1366 Petrarch for instance, referred to the Alps as 'the soaring mountains set against the fury of the barbarians.'

It is the paradox of her history during the Middle Ages and Renaissance that Italy presents an extraordinarily flourishing commercial situation against a chaotic political background. Probably both commercial wealth and political divisions were responsible for the development of the 'civilisation of the Renaissance in Italy', but conditions varied from city to city, and circumstances of course changed throughout the period covered by this book. It is impossible to tell exactly to what extent the production of art depended on the great wealth at Italian patrons' disposal, and how much it was stimulated by political and social rivalries.

Certainly Italy throughout the present period was rich beyond comparison with the North, for Italian merchants were closest to the eastern sources of luxury goods such as spices and silks which were so eagerly sought after by the rest of Europe. It is true that the discovery of fresh sea-routes to the East in the 15th century gradually changed the traditional pattern of trade, while the discovery of America and the flow of American gold and silver to the Spanish kingdom in turn affected the Italian economy; but the full consequences of these discoveries were not felt until the 17th century. From the 14th to the 16th centuries Italians remained the bankers of Europe *par excellence*, and dominated the luxury trade and commerce of the continent through a concentration of rich and flourishing towns—Genoa, Milan, Venice in the north; Mantua and Ferrara; Bologna and the towns of the Via Emilia; Florence, Pisa, Siena; and Perugia, the towns of the Papal States and Rome itself.

The causes of Italian political disunity are beyond the scope of this book, but the root of the trouble was undoubtedly the lack of any effective unifying authority. Nominally much of Italy belonged to the Holy Roman Emperors (successors to the Frankish Charlemagne for whom the title was revived in Rome in the year 800), but as Germans these emperors had never succeeded in effectively governing the whole peninsula, and in any case their claims to political domination were frequently resisted by the popes who undermined attempts at imperial organisation of Italy. In the early 14th century the great Italian poet Dante attributed most of the disorders of his native land to her political disunity in his treatise *On Monarchy*. In the middle of the century the Luxemburg emperor Charles IV (crowned

emperor 1355) recognised that even in northern Italy his own officials (such as the Visconti in Milan) only waited to increase their personal power and usurp what imperial rights were left.

Yet, in spite of hostility to foreign domination, Italians were never able to unite in repelling the outsiders as they crossed the Alpine passes; internal political divisions proliferated, and seem to have been increased by commercial rivalry. But during the 15th century Italy had some respite from foreign invasion, since the French kings had long been occupied in constant wars with the English, while the power of the German emperors—even in their own lands—was being constantly weakened by their own subjects. The historian can see that the invasion of Italy by the French king Charles VIII in 1494, and the German Sack of Rome in 1527, show the resumption of an earlier pattern of Italian history brought about by the consolidation of the French monarchy under Louis XI, and the rise of the house of Habsburg under the Emperor Maximilian (1493–1519); but to contemporary Italians these events were an enormous shock following the absence of serious threat from northern Europe during the earlier part of the 15th century. In retrospect this century seemed a 'Golden Age' mirrored by the artistic achievements to be described in this book.

Internally the first half of the 15th century saw the gradual crystallisation of the five great powers of Italy: Milan, Venice, Florence, Naples and the Papal States whose rulers drew within their orbits the rulers of lesser cities, or replaced them. A characteristic of this period is that the Italian princes developed what ultimately became the modern machinery of diplomacy based on a strong and—in many ways—civilised dislike for large-scale wars. Wherever possible they used highly trained mercenaries led by such men as Francesco Sforza and Bartolommeo Colleoni (commemorated by Verrocchio), and their reliance on such armies was accompanied by the development of diplomacy through the system of resident agents and representatives whose aims included the reduction in scope of any war and the erection of elaborate systems of alliances. These developments are perhaps summed up in a conversation recorded by the Florentine Machiavelli to whom the French cardinal de Rohan remarked that the Italians did not understand war, whereupon Machiavelli replied that the French did not understand politics (*The Prince*, chapter III).

The concentration of wealth and the competing centres of political power led also to an exceptional concentration of different artistic centres (in striking contrast to conditions north of the Alps) and, throughout the period, the possession of power and wealth was invariably accompanied by ostentatious display, at its most ephemeral in court festivities, processions and pageants, but often lastingly commemorated in public and family palaces, *mausolea*, and in all the decorative fittings executed for prince-citizens like the bankers Cosimo and Lorenzo de' Medici. Almost invariably great rulers in Italy were also great patrons.

2. **Andrea del Verrocchio.** *Equestrian statue of Bartolommeo Colleoni.* 1481–8. Bronze. Venice. Bartolommeo Colleoni came from a Bergamasque family and commanded the forces of the Venetian republic between 1455 and his death in 1475. Leaving a large part of his private fortune to the republic, he also stipulated that they should erect a public monument to him. The result was the figure begun by Andrea del Verrocchio.

3. **Sandro Botticelli.** *Giuliano de' Medici. c.* 1475. Paint on panel. 21¼ × 14¼ in. (54 × 36 cm.). Staatliche Museen, Berlin. Five years younger than his famous brother, Lorenzo the Magnificent, Giuliano was murdered in the cathedral of Florence during the Pazzi conspiracy (1478). Like his brother, he was a patron of letters and the arts.

The renaissance of interest and enthusiasm for the language, philosophy and literature of antiquity began as a largely academic movement in the 14th century; various cities such as Florence then became centres of the 'humanistic' philosophy which scholars evolved from their pagan classical sources; eventually the humanists and their ideas had a considerable effect on the visual arts. In particular, the study of antique texts like Plutarch's *Lives* seems to have transformed the way in which men regarded their contemporaries—or at least the way in which historians wrote about them. A work like the *Lives* stresses the character of the 'great man', and undoubtedly helped to foster the cult of the individual in 15th-century Italy, so that biographical and autobiographical writing became increasingly fashionable. The Florentine bookseller Vespasiano di Bisticci, who was acquainted with a wide variety of eminent men, wrote his own *Lives*, and it is surely significant that the lives of two northern artists, Roger van der Weyden and Jan van Eyck, were first written by an Italian scholar, Bartolommeo Fazio, between 1453 and 1457. Machiavelli's *Prince* was written as an invocation to the inept Lorenzo II de' Medici to become a 'great man' and rid Italy of the 'festering sore' of barbarian invaders. The task undertaken by Vasari in his *Lives* (1550 and, enlarged, 1568) shows this cult of the individual being applied to the careers of painters, as well as to men of illustrious political houses; and there is no doubt that the emphasis on the importance of the individual, the influence of his actions and personal foibles, gives Italian history a human dimension which no other contemporary society possesses. To some extent, on the other hand, the acceptance by writers and men of importance of an individual for his personal achievements (and not solely for his investiture with office, or because of his hereditary importance) probably provided Italian artists with a more liberal background than their northern counterparts.

The devotion of scholars to the recovery of classical writings and the imitation of classical language and style also paved the way for any revival of antique art: and, because this was an academic movement, it acquired a prestige which it would otherwise not have had and, moreover, gained a widespread currency since the scholars were the most articulate members of society. The exact process by which practising sculptors, painters and masons became conscious of this classical literary revival cannot now be traced; but it was certainly assisted by the additional visual stimulus in the plentiful classical monuments which survived in their country. It is certainly significant that in the early 15th century artists such as Brunelleschi went to Rome to study and to ponder on the classical ruins there.

At this point, it might be tempting to interpret the course of Italian 15th-century artistic development in a way similar to that of literature and letters; and to postulate a similar 'Renaissance' associated with attempts to recover a shattered but not entirely vanished heritage from the antique world of Greece and Rome. The situation, however, was far more complicated. Indeed, it is possible that the concept of 'Renaissance' is a hindrance to understanding since it associates the production of art with a somewhat artificial scheme of progress in which the worth of any work is measured by the extent to which it looks 'classical' or 'antique'. This attitude gives whole tracts of art history the appearance of stagnation, particularly north of the Alps, and destroys the idea of continuity in Italian art itself by discounting those elements which bind the art to its immediate past. Such an idea also gives a false impression of the artists concerned as being merely painstaking archaeologists rather than creative individuals.

To avoid distortions of this nature the opening chapter of this book is concerned with 'change' rather than 'Renaissance'. The theme of change is, of course, generally common to all art at all times. But in Europe (1400) there occurred one of those rare moments of community of artistic expression between Italy and the North which gave subsequent changes something of the nature of a common point of departure, summed up by the expression 'International Gothic art'. Taking this style as a starting point, it will be easier to compare Italian to other European art, and to understand more clearly the character of what is normally called the art of the early Renaissance.

THE INTERNATIONAL STYLE

This phrase was never intended to imply that art produced north and south of the Alps looked identical. Common features, however, can certainly be found in works produced for the most important artistic centres of the time which justify its use. In art produced for the courts of Paris, Prague and Milan (three of the most important centres of patronage) the general Gothic figure style of the 14th century persisted. This meant that figures were elegant, sometimes rather mannered, portrayed without passion and that drapery was decorative. Moreover, this figure style was associated with a narrative style which was frequently anecdotal and discursive; and works of art often contained a lavish display of fashionable costume and rich ornament and a wealth of incidental detail such as animals and flowers wherever the artist could find space to include these.

There can be little doubt that the introduction of such detail and the general decorative effect for which artists strove corresponded with their patrons' tastes. But the striking quality of work produced in this style must also always have depended on the enthusiasm and interest of the patrons involved and, in this respect, the artists of both Bohemia and France were particularly fortunate. In Bohemia the emperors Charles IV (1346–1378) and Wenzel IV (1378–1419) were both ardent patrons of the arts; while in France, the French royal family included such well-known connoisseurs as Charles V (1364–1380) and his brothers Philip the Bold, Duke of Burgundy (died 1404) and John, Duke of Berry (died 1416).

There were differences in the appearance of art produced in northern Europe. The pictorial style current in Prague

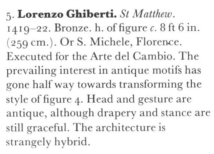

4. **Lorenzo Ghiberti.** *St John the Baptist.*
1414. Bronze. h. of figure 8 ft (244 cm.).
Or S. Michele, Florence. Executed for the
Arte dei Mercanti. This was Ghiberti's
first important surviving commission to be
completed. By Italian standards
(compare figure 11) this is an unusually
graceful figure much influenced by the
International Gothic style (compare
figure 18).

5. **Lorenzo Ghiberti.** *St Matthew.*
1419–22. Bronze. h. of figure *c.* 8 ft 6 in.
(259 cm.). Or S. Michele, Florence.
Executed for the Arte del Cambio. The
prevailing interest in antique motifs has
gone half way towards transforming the
style of figure 4. Head and gesture are
antique, although drapery and stance are
still graceful. The architecture is
strangely hybrid.

6. **Nicolo di Piero Lamberti (il Pela).**
St Luke. c. 1400. Marble. Museo Nazionale,
Florence. Formerly on Or S. Michele.
Executed for the Arte dei Giudici e Notai.
Nicolo was not an outstanding master but
his *St Luke* shows well the style perpetuated
in Florence since the early 14th century
(compare Andrea Pisano)—a stolid figure
covered by many small neat drapery folds.

had a gently modelled appearance from which it has acquired the name 'the soft style'. It became popular ultimately in much of what is now modern Germany, from Hamburg in the north to Swabia in the south, and along the Rhine where the city of Cologne formed an important centre. The 'soft style' is still to be seen in the work of Stefan Lochner of Cologne during the 1440s. The rather heavy rounded Bohemian style never made very serious headway in Paris, for the surviving panel paintings and manuscripts suggest that the French royal family as a rule favoured a more refined and elegant technique. The Dukes of Milan appear to have favoured both styles although the history of Milanese court art is by no means clear.

The spread of this stylistic fashion southwards into Italy was slow and complicated but there are unmistakable signs of its presence and popularity in Florence between 1390 and 1425. In Florence, the painter Lorenzo Monaco was a gifted exponent of it by the end of his life (*c.* 1370–*c.* 1425); and Gentile da Fabriano brought the style, with all its richness and delicacy, with him when he came south to Florence (*c.* 1421). It may be observed that Gentile was a true court artist who had worked in the ducal palace at

Venice and was to go on to work for the papal court in Rome (*c.* 1427).

Another admirer of these characteristics was the Florentine sculptor Lorenzo Ghiberti. In fact, no other Florentine sculptor of the period imitated with such incisive elegance this late Gothic style from the North. At the start of his career (1401) he was confronted by the famous competition for the commission of a pair of bronze doors for the Florentine baptistery. Ghiberti gained the commission after submitting a bronze relief on the subject of the *Sacrifice of Isaac*. His relief and one other by the Florentine Brunelleschi are all that remain from the competition but they show that these two competitors were working in totally different styles; and of the two, it is surely significant that the Florentine judges preferred the Gothic elegance of Ghiberti's work. For, whereas Brunelleschi emphasised above all the drama and tragedy of this Old Testament scene, Ghiberti paid more attention to its surface finish. His torso of Isaac is a beautiful piece of modelling and his Abraham is clothed in a delicate ripple of folds. The qualities found in Ghiberti's relief were developed by him in his first pair of bronze doors. The figure style is also to be

seen in his first great bronze statue for Or S. Michele—the
4 *St John the Baptist* of 1414. Ghiberti's position, however, is
far more ambiguous than that of the painters who worked
in this late Gothic style; and although his figure style remained essentially the same throughout his long career (he
died in 1455), his sculpture on occasions reveals the characteristics of the more forceful and expressive style which
superseded the decorative elegance of the 'International
Gothic'.

ARTISTIC CHANGE IN TUSCANY

It is apparent that many artists in Tuscany were not satis-
fied with this late Gothic style. Indeed, as early as 1401
3 Brunelleschi's trial relief provides evidence of a revolt
against these decorative conventions. The attention given
by Brunelleschi to the modelling of the torso of Isaac is so
summary as to provide a strong contrast to Ghiberti's
work. Isaac's body is distorted and great emphasis is laid
on Abraham's dramatic gesture as he is about to sacrifice
11-14 his child. Other sculptors followed this lead, notably
7 Donatello and Nanni di Banco in Florence, and the rather
9 isolated figure of Jacopo della Quercia in Siena; and all
successfully produced individual solutions to their common
problem of exploring some form of artistic expression which
avoided the elegant superficiality of much of the work of
their contemporaries and immediate predecessors.

To what sources did these men turn in their search for an
art which was more serious and visually more dramatic?
Since no artist at this date recorded his intentions or im-
pressions, it is only possible to answer this question from a
consideration of the sculptors' actual work. It here becomes apparent that one important influence was not a
classical source at all but the work of an earlier Tuscan
8 sculptor, Giovanni Pisano, perhaps the most dramatic and
passionate sculptor of the entire early Gothic period. Admittedly Giovanni Pisano never actually worked in Florence, but he left two major monuments nearby, the façade
sculpture on Siena cathedral and the pulpit of S. Andrea
at Pistoia. Here at hand were violent dramatic gestures,
deeply cut expressive drapery and, indeed, that impa-
tience with surface texture as an end in itself, which are so
apparent in the Brunelleschi relief by comparison with
Ghiberti's work.

It seems probable, therefore, that sculptors deliberately
turned back to art of the not-so-distant past in search of
qualities which they could not find in the work of their
masters or contemporaries. A similar process may be found
in Florentine painting at a slightly later date when
6 Masaccio ignored current stylistic tendencies and produced
work whose gravity and indeed austerity can only have
come from a very penetrating appraisal of the art of Giotto.
Thus it seems to have been the work of medieval rather
than classical artists which at first stimulated Tuscan
sculptors and painters to rebel against the accepted artistic
conventions of the late 14th century.

Nevertheless, the development of art in Italy has always

7. **Nanni di Banco.** *Virgin of the Assumption.* 1414–21. Marble.
On the Porta della Mandorla, Duomo, Florence. Nanni di
Banco was a remarkable experimenter, changing to this excited,
vigorous style from the absolute impassiveness of the *Quattro
Santi Coronati* figures. His work, so unlike that of Ghiberti,
shows again the immense stylistic upheaval of the early
15th century in Florence.

been complicated by the visible remains of the classical
world. Not unnaturally, sculptors were particularly affected by these remains since architecture and sculpture survived in comparatively large quantities whereas the painting had virtually all perished. Thus throughout the Middle
Ages, Italian sculptors continued to imitate classical decorative motifs and showed a general preference for relief
sculpture—a typically classical form. Indeed, the first great
Tuscan Gothic sculptor, Nicola Pisano, was already drawing heavily from antiquity in the 13th century, so that in
the early 15th century, during the first stylistic upheaval
since that period, it comes as no surprise to find sculptors
once more turning to antique art in search of inspiration.

But in Italy in 1400 this change coincided with the literary and humanistic movement already mentioned. The
Florentines, building on foundations laid in the 14th century by Petrarch, came positively to identify themselves
with the republicanism of ancient Rome in their military
struggle against the presumed tyranny of the Visconti
Dukes of Milan. Politics and scholarship were actually
linked in the persons of two successive and remarkable
chancellors of Florence, Coluccio Salutati (chancellor

8. **Giovanni Pisano.** *A Sybil.* 1297–1301. Marble. h. 24½ in. (62 cm.). On the pulpit, S. Andrea, Pistoia. Giovanni Pisano evolved one of the most dramatic interpretations of Gothic style. His figures were full of expression and movement, of a type to be found in work by Jacopo della Quercia (see figure 9).

9. **Jacopo della Quercia.** *Figure representing a Virtue.* 1414–19. Marble. Fragment from the Fonte Gaia, now in the Palazzo Pubblico, Siena. Jacopo used figures such as this to animate the architecture of the huge fountain called the Fonte Gaia. Characteristic of this animating movement is the extreme turn of the figure whereby the head points in one direction and the knees another.

1375–1406) and Leonardo Bruni (chancellor 1411–1444).

It is difficult to know what importance this literary movement had for those Florentines who were not scholars. The finer points of the new academic teaching must have been beyond the grasp of all but a small minority. There is, however, plenty of evidence to suggest that the emulation of antiquity was, at the very least, a fashionable attitude which was within the reach of everyone. A man might not be very clear about republican virtues or the teaching of Cicero; but the identification of Florence as the heir of ancient Rome in the cause of liberty could be as much a matter of the heart as of the head.

From this, however, it follows that it is much harder to estimate the significance which this 'classical revival' had for working artists. Certainly during the first twenty years of the century many seem increasingly to have used ideas which are recognisably classical in origin. Two instances occur: in the trial reliefs already described Brunelleschi used the classical statue of the *Spinario*, the boy taking a thorn from his foot, as the basis for one of his lower figures; but Brunelleschi's version is swathed with Gothic drapery in such a way as to transform the original model of a naked boy. Ghiberti's figure of Isaac is also based on an antique model. The artist here showed a remarkable sensitivity to the nuances of classical flesh modelling and it is thus curious that the more 'Gothic' artist had a far greater *rapport* with his classical original.

Although these provide instances of detailed borrowing from antique art, the reliefs could hardly be described as antique in appearance. However, there were also a number of far more remarkable essays in a classical style, particularly in the niche figures on the church of Or S. Michele. In the statues of the *Quattro Santi Coronati* the sculptor, Nanni di Banco, emulated a Roman style in some of the drapery, and some of the heads are based on classical busts of a type similar to those representing Caracalla. Yet the whole group still has only a superficially antique appearance, for the drapery style is not consistent in its classicism and the whole group is contained in a niche that is solidly and ornately Gothic. Moreover, along the base is a relief scene carved in an unremarkable traditional manner.

It is clear from Nanni di Banco's development that he was not concerned with what might be called an organised classical revival. Both he and Donatello were eclectics in the best sense of the word, choosing from and experimenting with what they saw around them, and antique models were far from being their chief or unique source of inspiration. Ghiberti's work also shows a similar eclecticism and a very interesting example occurs in his statue of St Matthew on Or S. Michele. This figure shows that Ghiberti too had been affected by the expressive qualities which other sculptors had already seen in antique figures and his sculpture momentarily acquired a rhetorical feeling which on the whole is alien to his style. The hybrid nature of the whole conception, however, is clear. The triangular pediment of the niche, the fluted pilasters, the eloquent gesture and the modelling of the head derive from antique models. But the crockets climbing up the pediment, the pointed arch, the sway of St Matthew's figure and the sweep of drapery clearly recall how close to the surface Ghiberti's Gothic antecedents are.

The direct imitation of antiquity proceeded so erratically that it cannot be supposed that the artists themselves saw the recovery of antiquity as a species of mission to which they were bound. But scholars, already heavily saturated with an admiration of antiquity, were very soon prepared to explain the artistic revolution which they had witnessed in terms of the recovery—or renaissance—of an art that had been lost since the decline of the Roman Empire. The idea of a 'renaissance' in art achieved its universal acceptance precisely because it was the explanation placed on events by the existing *litterati*, the scholars and historians. Ultimately the main historian chiefly responsible for this interpretation was probably Giorgio Vasari, a painter with a humanist education, whose great work *The Lives of the Most Excellent Italian Architects, Painters and Sculptors* appeared in the mid-16th century. Long before this time, however, the legend of the 'Renaissance of classical antiquity' had been born.

It had comparatively innocent beginnings, in that early 15th-century humanists found it complimentary to compare the greatness that they knew from experience with the greatness that they knew only from literary tradition. In this fashion the 15th-century renown even of Gentile da Fabriano was compared with the ancient renown of Greek artists such as Apelles, Parrhasius and Zeuxis. There was, however, perilously small distinction between this comparison of the *renown* of the ancients and moderns and a comparison of the *achievements* of the two civilisations. From there it was a small step to suggesting that the achievements of the present were rendered possible by a recovery of those of the past, and that the past was 'reborn' in the present.

This chain of reasoning was encouraged by 15th-century developments in Italian historiography where the idea of a 'middle age' of destruction or stagnation was now postulated. It was this historiographical framework that Ghiberti adopted when he came, late in life (*c.* 1450), to write three *Commentarii* in which he attempted the highly personal task of placing his own achievements in an his-

10. **Nanni di Banco.** *The Quattro Santi Coronati. c.* 1415. Marble. Or S. Michele, Florence. Perhaps the only obvious stylistic link between this niche and figure 7 lies in the figure of the blessing Christ in the gable. Although the niche is in general character similar to that of figure 4, the evidence of interest in antique art is very strong in the heads which are based on different antique types. Executed for the Arte dei Fabbri.

11. **Donatello.** *St Louis. c.* 1423. Gilt bronze. h. 104¾ in.
(266 cm.). Here seen in its original niche on Or S. Michele,
Florence. Now in Museo dell'Opera di S. Croce, Florence.
Executed for the Guelphs. The weighty folds of the drapery
betray a style completely different from that of Ghiberti. No
less striking is the architecture of the niche, far more faithful
to the art of antiquity than the niche of *St Matthew* which
immediately preceded it (figure 5).

torical setting. Art history fell into three main divisions.
Ghiberti first dealt with antique art in large sections of text
lifted directly from Vitruvius and Pliny; there followed a
very short section on the 'middle age' followed in turn by
the 'revival' of art *c.* 1300. This revival, of course, cul-
minates in Ghiberti's own life and work. But Ghiberti's
historical standpoint, even in imitating contemporary
practice, provides a further warning against a too rigid
conception of a 'Renaissance' in Italian art *c.* 1400. The
revival described by Ghiberti was one of art as a whole
c. 1300. What interested him was the age of Giotto and the
development of Gothic art out of the previous Italo-Byzan-
tine style, a development to which he attached his own
career. Although himself an interested collector of antique
sculpture, the literal recovery of an antique style is never
mentioned as a legitimate or significant factor in Tuscan
developments. Again, for artists themselves, classical antiquity was only one of a number of sources or aids to
change; at this stage the 'Renaissance' did not have for
them the status of an artistic programme or manifesto.

The impression is strengthened therefore that developments in Florentine art *c.* 1400–25 represent, not an attempt to recover antiquity, but a reinterpretation of a
number of existing elements which included the visible
remains from the High Gothic period *c.* 1300 as well as the
classical past. The result was a new style at once powerful,
dramatic and rich in variation. Brunelleschi's trial relief
pointed in this direction; but the most violent expression
of this change is to be found in the work of Donatello. This
is easily seen in the series of standing figures, devised for
the campanile of Florence cathedral and for the church of
Or S. Michele. They include an evangelist, *St Mark*; a
warrior saint, *St George*; an episcopal saint, *St Louis of*   11
Toulouse; and a group of prophets. Each in its own way is
a work of vivid imagination. Even the figure of *St Louis*,
traditionally a mild figure, is swathed in a heavy majestic
cope which lends the mild face a considerable gravity. The
standing prophets in the niches on the campanile show   12
how Donatello could re-think a traditional task of the
sculptor and imbue his statues with contrasted drapery and
varying emotional states.

Like his great predecessor Giovanni Pisano, Donatello
instilled dramatic force and vigour into almost every commission. He took up the motif of the naked *putto*, reintro-   14
duced earlier from antiquity by Jacopo della Quercia as a
decorative idea, but produced in two pulpit balustrades a
mob of running and jostling *putti* totally without precedent.
His treatment of a commission for some bronze doors in the   13
Old Sacristy of S. Lorenzo (Florence) was equally characteristic. Asked for doors whose panels should contain
pairs of prophets and apostles, he produced an individual
scheme for each panel so that the figures either salute each
other, argue, or almost pointedly seem to ignore each
other.

It is not difficult to appreciate that dramatic changes
occurred in Donatello's sculpture. The positive aspect of

12. **Donatello.** *Lo Zuccone.* 1427–36. Marble. h. 76¾ in.
(195 cm.). Museo dell'Opera del Duomo, Florence. Formerly
on the campanile. Heavy tumbling drapery and strong facial
characterisation are to be found in Donatello's statues for the
Florentine campanile. The dramatic use of drapery is again
reminiscent of Giovanni Pisano.

change in architecture can also be seen in the work of
Donatello's friend Brunelleschi from *c.* 1420. Brunelleschi,
like Donatello, had been trained as a goldsmith, but he was
probably ten years older than the sculptor. For some
reason architecture attracted him, and he became both an
engineer and a designer of buildings, perhaps under the
inspiration of a visit to Rome some time during the first two
decades of the century. Brunelleschi's first great achievement was the dome built over the crossing of Florence   15
cathedral—an engineering feat which involved the architect in the invention of an ingenious system of scaffolding
and in a complicated method of brick construction. The
latter was certainly in part derived from a study of Roman
ruins. The appearance of the dome, however, is certainly
not classical: it is supported on ribs and for technical
reasons has a distinctive, elongated shape unlike any dome
surviving from the antique world.

Brunelleschi also studied the details of classical monuments and it is generally assumed that he passed on to
Donatello the knowledge acquired from these investiga-
tions for, from about 1420, a number of comparatively
correct features drawn from antique architecture appear in
the sculptor's work. Perhaps the most striking instance of
this is the niche designed for the figure of *St Louis* on the   11
Or S. Michele. It takes little effort to realise the great difference between this and Ghiberti's niche for his *St Matthew*.   5
The only explanation is that somebody (probably Brunelleschi) had been looking very closely at antique niches
with the eye of an archaeologically minded draughtsman.

Nevertheless, in terms of classicism there is in Brunelleschi's architecture a hiatus between the engineering
aspect, the aspect of its detailed decoration and the overall
planning and impression. The dome of Florence cathedral,
as a mass of engineering, is conceived on a scale comparable
to the vast ruins in Rome. The detail of Brunelleschi's
buildings is probably more 'classical' than anything since
the end of the Roman Empire. But his style is as personal
as that of Donatello and Masaccio and, like theirs, must be
derived from a complex of sources which includes Tuscan
work from the not-so-distant past. For instance, it has frequently been remarked that the extensive use of coloured
marble and the light round-headed arcades which are particular features of Brunelleschi's style are also a constant
feature of Tuscan Romanesque architecture of the 12th
century (see S. Miniato al Monte, Florence).

Brunelleschi would certainly have admired the Romanesque architecture of Florence. The exact age of these
buildings was not known with any certainty and the baptistery, for instance, was widely thought to have been a
Roman temple. Even if he thought that these buildings
were late antique, however, Brunelleschi was still exercis-
ing a deliberate choice in their favour: for Early Christian
basilicas existed in Rome and it is clear that he rejected

(Continued on page 33)

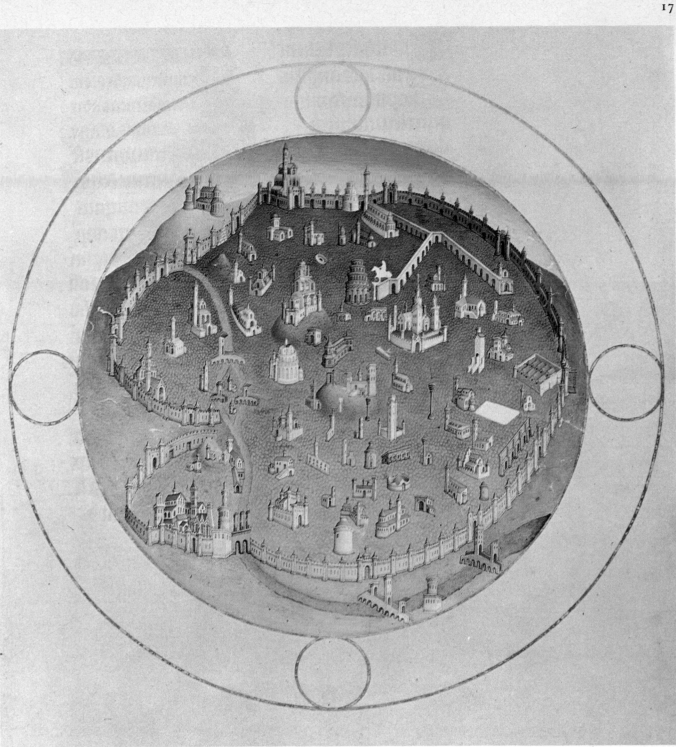

1. **The Limbourg Brothers.** *The City of Rome. c.* 1415. Painting on vellum. Page 11½ × 8¼ in. (29 × 21 cm.). From the *Très Riches Heures du Duc de Berry.* Musée Condé, Chantilly. Rome of the Middle Ages, city of marvels and travellers' tales. This is not strictly a northerner's account since, although the Limbourg brothers were Flemish, they seem here to have copied an Italian model. But, from what-ever source, the Rome of the sightseer is here clearly in evidence. The Vatican city (bottom, left), the Pantheon (left, centre) and the equestrian statue of Constantine (top right), then outside the Lateran palace, are easily visible. The history of Renaissance art is in part concerned with the change of attitude towards the visible remains of antiquity.

2. **Lorenzo Ghiberti.** *The Sacrifice of Isaac.* 1401. Bronze, parcel-gilt. 18 × 16 in. (46 × 41 cm.). Museo Nazionale, Florence. A trial relief submitted in the competition for the commission of a pair of bronze doors for the Florentine Baptistery. Comparison with the Brunelleschi relief below will establish through the common elements many of the detailed requirements of the competition. Ghiberti's composition is probably more subtle than that of Brunelleschi but the real difference lies in the emotional tone. Ghiberti's relief is remarkable for its refinement and delicacy, the dramatic elements being kept carefully in control.

3. **Filippo Brunelleschi.** *The Sacrifice of Isaac.* 1401. Bronze, parcel-gilt. 18 × 16 in. (46 × 41 cm.). Museo Nazionale, Florence. Produced in circumstances similar to Ghiberti's relief (above). By contrast, Brunelleschi paid very little attention to the beauty of the individual parts of the composition; compare, for instance, the two versions of the torso of Isaac. Brunelleschi produced a dramatic effect almost totally absent from Ghiberti's relief which permeates not merely the distorted figure of Isaac but also the deep folds of Abraham's cloak.

4. **Masaccio.** *St Peter healing the Sick by the Fall of his Shadow.* 1427. Fresco. 90½ × 63¾ in. (230 × 162 cm.). Brancacci Chapel, Sta Maria del Carmine, Florence. During his short life, much of Masaccio's most important work was done for the church of the Carmine. This scene reminds one how little he owed to the decorative and graceful work of many of his contemporaries. It is, however, equally far from the dramatic violence of Brunelleschi or Donatello, and much of Masaccio's ability to convey a situation through the telling glance or gesture seems to be derived from a new appreciation of Giotto.

5. **Lorenzo Monaco.** *Madonna and Child.*
c. 1410. Tempera on wood. Centre panel
of the Monte Oliveto altarpiece. Palazzo
Davanzati, Florence. One of the most
accomplished Florentine artists up to his
death in *c.* 1425–6; a friend and
associate of Ghiberti. The decorative
effect of this panel is self-evident. The
artist has, without making the figures
physically improbable, arranged the folds
of drapery in a series of loops and curls
which can be appreciated as a continuous
pattern. Depth and volume are minimised
to this end, and the figures are given a
conscious grace and elegance.

6. **Masaccio.** *Virgin and Child with Angels.*
1426. Tempera on wood. 53¼ × 28¾ in.
(135·5 × 73 cm.). National Gallery,
London. Central panel of a large
polyptych executed for Sta Maria del
Carmine, Pisa. An imposing ensemble
with no pretension to grace or elegance.
Space and volume are emphasised where
possible in order to heighten the subjective impression of physical presence.
Notable is the treatment of haloes which
now appear as foreshortened discs.

7. **Filippo Brunelleschi.** *The Old Sacristy, S. Lorenzo*, Florence. 1418–28. The use of coloured marble for decorative ends had long been a feature of Florentine architecture. In spite of the precise archaeological derivation of most of the detail, the Old Sacristy represents a brilliant rethinking of this tradition. The treatment of wall surfaces was still characteristically two-dimensional, and the heavy projecting pediments and columns of the twin entrances were probably additions of Donatello, whose doors they frame. Verrocchio's Medici tomb (left) with its arch was completed in 1472.

8. **Filippo Brunelleschi.** *S. Spirito*, Florence. The Nave looking east. Begun *c.* 1436. Although very similar to the earlier church of S. Lorenzo, S. Spirito contains several important changes. The general proportions of the component parts of the building were significantly altered. Furthermore the rectangular lines of the older church were modified by the addition of a string of apsidal chapels which encircle the church. In this way the architect moulded the internal contours of the church into something more interesting and more complicated.

THE PICTORIAL RELIEF IN THE
EARLY 15TH CENTURY

9. **Donatello.** *Herod's Feast and the
Execution of St John the Baptist.* 1427. Gilt
bronze. 23½ × 24 in. (60 × 61 cm.).
Relief from the font, Siena Baptistery.
10. **Lorenzo Ghiberti.** *The Story of
Jacob and Esau.* c. 1435. Gilt bronze.
31 × 31 in. (79 × 79 cm.). *Porta del
Paradiso*, Florence Baptistery. The device
of linear perspective benefited sculptors
as well as painters and the result was a
revived interest in the pictorial relief in
which a space deeper than the actual
depth of the carving was indicated
illusionistically. Like the painters, the
sculptors were enabled to control with
greater ease the relative sizes of
architecture and figures, as these examples
in sharply contrasted styles show.

11. The Circle of the Master of the Parement de Narbonne. *The Adoration of the Magi. c.* 1380. From the *Très Belles Heures du Duc de Berry*. Painting on vellum.

$11\frac{1}{2} \times 8\frac{1}{4}$ in. (29 × 21 cm.). Bibliothèque Nationale, Paris. This scene, from a sumptuous late 14th-century Book of Hours, is in style uncharacteristic of French book illumination, particularly in the large, serious, heavily modelled

heads of the figures (compare the following illustrations). This feature derives from Italy, but other more enduring aspects of Italian influence are visible, particularly in the construction and control of pictorial space.

12. The Limbourg Brothers. *The Adoration of the Magi. c.* 1415. From the *Très Riches Heures du Duc de Berry.* Painting on vellum. Page 11½ × 8¼ in. (29 × 21 cm.). Musée Condé, Chantilly.

An extravagant full-page spread of fascinating detail. The modelling of the facial features is scarcely emphasised and figures have a grace and elegance lacking in plate 11. Yet in order to amass so much detail the artists had to know how to construct the space of a landscape, and this understanding came from Italy.

13. **The Master of the Hours of the Maréchal de Boucicaut.** *The Flight into Egypt. c.* 1405–10. From the *Hours of the Maréchal de Boucicaut.* Painting on vellum. Page 10¾ × 7½ in. (27·5 × 19 cm.). Musée Jacquemart-André, Paris. This Book of Hours is striking, among other things, for its landscape settings. In their European context they are remarkable since the artist has departed so far from the conventional treatment of rock-formations and attempted also to indicate an atmospheric haze in the far distance.

14. **Melchior Broederlam.** *The Annunciation.* After 1392. Wing from an altarpiece executed for Philip the Bold, Duke of Burgundy, originally in the Chartreuse de Champmol, Dijon. Painting on wood. 63¾ × 51¼ in. (162 × 130 cm.). Dijon Museum. The scene takes place in a palace, replete with symbolism but also containing elaborate decoration, a smart tiled floor and a pretty garden. To the right are the traditional rock-formations used to indicate landscape (compare plate 13). This ambitious spatial construction is a further instance of the influence of Italian example but the restraint and delicacy of the figures are typical of French taste.

15. **Robert Campin.** *The Annunciation. c.* 1425. Centre panel of the Mérode triptych. Painting on wood. 25½ × 25½ in. (64·5 × 64·5 cm.). Cloisters Collection, Metropolitan Museum of Art, New York. Painted for the Inghelbrecht family of Malines, Belgium, this interpretation of the theme is remarkable for the setting in which it takes place. There is, again, much implied symbolism in the detail, but the completeness of the interior setting and the unpretentious *milieu* are new features in Flemish panel-painting. The full rounded faces stand in contrast to those of Broederlam, and are reminiscent of the style of plate 11. Also clearly visible here is the new angular drapery convention which made its appearance *c.* 1420.

THE PORTRAYAL OF EMOTION,
OLD AND NEW STYLE

16. *Pietà. c.* 1400. Painting on panel.
Diameter 25¼ in. (64 cm.). Louvre, Paris.
Like plate 14, this was executed for

Philip, Duke of Burgundy and has been
attributed to Jean Malouel, court artist
and probably the uncle of the Limbourg
brothers (see plates 1 and 12). It is a
sensitive and moving composition,
depending very little on facial expression

to achieve the impression of tragedy and
grief. This reticence seems to have been a
general characteristic of French court
taste.

17. **Roger van der Weyden.** *The Descent from the Cross. c.* 1435. Painting on panel. 78¾ × 104¼ in. (200 × 265 cm.). Prado, Madrid. Painted for the chapel of the Guild of Archers, Louvain. The desire of the painter to involve the spectator directly in the tragedy of the occasion is clear and contrasts strongly with plate 16. Facial expression is important and gestures and actions are more dramatic, the figures being placed as if on a stage.

18 (opposite). **Hubert** and **Jan van Eyck.**
The Ghent altarpiece (lower scenes, front
face). Completed 1432. Painting on panel.
Dimensions of *The Adoration of the Lamb*
(above) 4 ft 5¾ in. × 7 ft 11½ in.
(136·5 × 242 cm.). Panels below, each
4 ft 10 in. × 1 ft 8¼ in. (147 × 51 cm.).
St Bavon, Ghent. The nature of Hubert's
contribution has never been unanimously
agreed. These five panels (the largest is
actually set in the centre of the four
narrower ones) illustrate the enlarged
scale of the painter's conception of settings.
Like a great wall-painting, this landscape
may be read continuously from one side
to the other.

19. **Roger van der Weyden.** *The
Entombment. c.* 1450. Painting on panel.
14 × 17¾ in. (35·5 × 45 cm.). Louvre,
Paris. In comparison with plate 17 it is
clear that the more extrovert aspects of
grief have been quietly laid on one side.
Only the symbolism of grief is retained in
the attitude of the kneeling Magdalen.
This gesture and the scheme as a whole
were probably noted by Roger during a
visit to Italy in 1450 (the basis of the
composition seems to be a work of Fra
Angelico) but the style of their restate-
ment is totally northern. This makes an
interesting contrast to later attitudes in
the North to Italian art.

20. **Jan van Eyck.** *The Madonna with the
Chancellor Rolin. c.* 1435. Painting on panel.
26 × 24½ in. (66 × 62 cm.). Louvre,
Paris. The cardinal Rolin was chancellor
of the duke of Burgundy and the
splendour of the setting of this votive
painting reflects his social standing.
(Compare plate 15, where the kneeling
donor appears on a side panel, not
included here). This is one of Jan van
Eyck's most brilliant works, displaying
his gift for portraiture and his astounding
technique as a painter of detail and
texture.

them as models for his main churches since they had one particular decorative feature which Brunelleschi ignored. They made extensive use of fresco cycles on the walls. This decorative fashion had spread to Tuscany. A certain amount of mosaic decoration appears in the baptistery of Florence; and frescoes were added to the aisle walls of S. Miniato. But the main decorative effect in those churches came overwhelmingly from the application of a marble incrustation to the walls.

Brunelleschi's turn towards this style of architecture is one of the more remarkable features of Florentine art at this time. To have imitated old St Peter's, Rome, with its great fresco cycles running along the walls above the main nave colonnade would have been perfectly permissible and genuinely 'antique'. Painters existed who could well have executed the paintings. Yet Brunelleschi deliberately planned buildings which excluded painted frescoes from their decorative scheme and, like the earlier Florentine churches, relied for their decorative effect on the handling of coloured marble. The reason can now only be guessed; but it is likely that these Tuscan buildings would have seemed to him more genuinely 'architect's churches' in which the architect was in complete charge from the start, planning and foreseeing every aspect of the completed effect. For this reason, the curious fact emerges that almost none of the great achievements of the 15th-century fresco painters in Florence was executed in a 15th-century building because the architectural fashion revived by Brunelleschi made no provision for this kind of decoration.

Brunelleschi certainly chose this style precisely because the entire completed effect of any architectural project mattered a great deal to him. In particular the mathematical relationship of one part of a church to another part, both in plan and in elevation, was worked out with great care; and in underlining shape and proportion the plain grey-green *pietra serena* of Florence undoubtedly plays a vital role. All Brunelleschi's buildings display an intricate system of interrelated proportions.

Brunelleschi's architectural style did not change very much. He experimented, however, in a number of different types of building—for instance, the loggia of the *Innocenti* or the two churches of S. Lorenzo and S. Spirito. Very important for the future were the more compact buildings such as the Old Sacristy (of S. Lorenzo) or the Pazzi chapel (of S. Croce). There was, however, one subtle and interesting development in Brunelleschi's feeling for the sculptural qualities of architecture. Much of his work is constructed of flat wall-surfaces articulated by *pietra serena* pilasters or ornament (the church of S. Lorenzo is an example). During the 1430s he appears to have discovered that the walls could, as it were, assume a shape of their own, and that an architect, in modelling the walls into convex or concave shapes, was also fashioning the interior space into something more complex and exciting. This change can be followed in S. Spirito or in the unfinished church of Sta Maria degli Angeli. It may be connected with a further

13. **Donatello.** *Bronze door* in the Old Sacristy, S. Lorenzo, Florence. Between 1434 and 1443. Bronze. 92½ × 43 in. (235 × 109 cm.). The problem of what to do with repeated pairs of figures was solved here in a most dramatic way. The summary nature of the dividing ornamental bands focusses attention on the action contained in the rectangles.

14. **Donatello.** *Cantoria.* 1433–8. Marble with polychrome mosaic inlay. Overall size 137 × 224½ in. (348 × 570 cm.). Museo dell'Opera del Duomo, Florence. Using an antique idea already revived by Jacopo della Quercia, Donatello enriched the balustrade of the gallery with this unruly mob of dancing *putti* who move as on a stage set behind the proscenium framework of the columns.

15. **Filippo Brunelleschi.** *The dome of Florence cathedral* from the south-east. Built *c.* 1420–36. Lantern designed 1436 but only built after 1446. The dome, of unusual shape, dominates the surrounding city and it is still possible to get a 15th-century impression of the gigantic nature of Brunelleschi's achievement. Much of the upper part is of concealed brick to lighten the structure.

journey to Rome which there is some reason to suppose that Brunelleschi took with Donatello in 1433. Certainly the plan of Sta Maria degli Angeli is very close to that of the Roman temple of Minerva Medica. Brunelleschi may therefore have become aware of the fact that much Roman imperial building makes its effect through the complicated shape of the walls as well as through the surface adornment.

The mathematics or geometry which Brunelleschi required in calculating his architectural effects also led him by paths now obscure to pioneer a carefully calculated system of perspective construction—that is, to devise a system for the representing of three-dimensional shapes on a flat surface by the use of geometrical constructions on the part of the painter. Only descriptions survive of his practical demonstrations of the new technique for calculating the recession of space on a flat surface; the codification of the method was made by the scholar Leone Battista Alberti in his treatise on painting of 1435. Sculptors were also interested in these problems and, about 1420, the pictorial relief was revived as a medium of art. Medieval relief sculpture as a rule had pretended to no greater depth than the actual depth of the stone carving; but now sculptors began to treat the area of the stone surface after the manner of a picture, modelling the figures against a complete and receding background which was generally indicated in a low, delicate relief. In carving of this type it was possible to give the new technique of perspective construction full play, as can be seen in the work of both Donatello and Ghiberti.

9
10

During these years Masaccio made his debut as a painter, being inscribed in the guild of the *Medici e Speziali* in January 1422. Born in 1401, Masaccio was far younger than either Brunelleschi or Donatello. The problem of his training as an artist has never been completely settled but he collaborated frequently with another artist from the same Florentine parish, Masolino. Since Masolino was the elder by almost twenty years his work might be expected to have had some effect on the young artist; yet curiously Masaccio's painting (with its economy, austerity and solidity) owes little, if anything, to Masolino's late Gothic style. Masaccio must somehow have acquired a distaste for the current decorative tendencies in painting, and this distaste must have led him to study the work of Giotto and also that of sculptors, past and present. Little exact imitation can be found in Masaccio's fragmentary surviving painting; but there is no other explanation for the extreme plasticity of his figures, otherwise extremely uncharacteristic of his period. His work must also have owed something to Brunelleschi, for Masaccio undoubtedly knew of the general developments taking place in the study of perspective as **16** can be seen from his huge fresco of *The Trinity* in Sta Maria Novella. Again from this fresco it can be seen that he must have been thoroughly acquainted with the elements of antique architecture.

In 1428 Masaccio went to Rome where he died within a few months. Two commissions from among his surviving works should be mentioned. The first was a polyptych, an altarpiece painted for the church of the Carmine in Pisa in 1426; the fragments of this are now dispersed throughout a number of different galleries, and the central figures **6** —*a Virgin and Child with Angels*—are in the National Gallery, London. In this it will be noticed that part of the solidity of Masaccio's figures comes from the painter's awareness of the part played by light and shadow in defining volume. The presence of the Virgin is also rendered more imposing by the device of a low viewpoint, while a number of supplementary features tend to stress both this viewpoint and the solidity of the figures. These include the projecting fingerboard of the lute played by the right-hand angel, but the most important is the halo of the Christ Child, painted not as the customary flat circle but as a solid, three-dimensional disc. The frescoes which he painted **4** in the Brancacci chapel of the Florentine Carmine church also contain these qualities. As might be expected, the general tone of the narrative is one of majestic gravity; the frescoes are sombre in expression, although an atmosphere of emotional tension is created by the hysterical pathos of Eve and the hopeless gesture of Adam as they are driven out of Eden.

All the known works of Masaccio represent the uncompromising style of a young man. Like most uncompromising works, his painting has a certain lack of appeal, for Masaccio was certainly not interested in conveying either charm or conventional beauty to the beholder. It is a matter of speculation whether, and in what directions, his style might have mellowed, had he lived.

At this period the phrase 'Italian Renaissance' is highly misleading if applied to the visual arts. As has already been suggested this is partly because artists were not yet themselves obsessed with the idea of a 'rebirth' of the greatness of classical antique art in their own works. But it should also be noticed that the artistic changes here described were in any case almost entirely restricted at first to Florence.

16. **Masaccio.** *The Trinity.* 1426–7. Fresco. 192½ × 124¾ in. (489 × 317 cm.). Sta Maria Novella, Florence. This fresco was painted as a funeral monument with those commemorated appearing as donors kneeling above an altar table. The gravity of the figures is matched by the enormous classical architectural setting which creates the impression of real physical presence in a way probably never before achieved by a painter.

For much of the first half of the 15th century the other important Italian centres of patronage—Venice, Verona, Ferrara or Milan for instance—continued to demand works which were essentially similar to those produced at the end of the 14th century. At this stage Florentine artistic change did not greatly affect the development of the visual arts in the rest of Italy.

ARTISTIC CHANGE IN FRANCE AND BOHEMIA

As in Tuscany major artists in the North were faced by the problem of developing, or breaking away from, the decorative conventions of the 'International Gothic' style. But, perhaps on account of disturbed political events, there was no continuity of development similar to that which is apparent in Florentine art. For in Prague conditions of court patronage became very unsettled following the deposition of the Emperor Wenzel in 1400 and, although Wenzel re-established himself and reigned as king in Bohemia until 1419, from 1400 onwards Prague became steadily less important as an artistic centre. In France the death of Charles VI in 1422 and the subsequent dynastic claims of the English king to the French crown led once more to war, and this temporarily eclipsed the artistic ascendancy of Paris. This lack of stability and continuity is tantalising for the historian of art because certain stylistic changes had already occurred in both these centres.

In Bohemia these changes took the form of an extra-ordinarily involved and mannered drapery and figure style which is difficult to describe, although easily recognisable (the *Madonna* of St Vitus, and the Krumlov *Madonna, c.* 1400). It appears to have been evolved shortly before 1400 and is to be found in the work of both painters and sculptors. In France, on the other hand, this style was confined to sculpture and is chiefly associated with the work of Claus Sluter, the *imagier* of the Duke of Burgundy.

Little is known about Sluter's origins, and some of his work is disputed, but changes similar to those found in the Bohemian figures can be observed in the *Virgin* (almost certainly from Sluter's hand) and in the portal figures at the entrance to the chapel of the Chartreuse de Champmol near Dijon. Here again the sculptor has breathed a new life into the conventions of the previous years, working the drapery into a fantastic cascade of folds but—and it is an important reservation—instilling his figures with a vigour and dramatic force without parallel in Bohemia. Sluter's individuality and originality has never been disputed and finds its most positive expression in the battered remains of a Calvary group, the so-called *Puits de Moïse*, which stands in the middle of the cloister of what was formerly the same Chartreuse. Now the base alone of this Calvary group survives intact: around its polygonal form stand figures of prophets, each swathed in voluminous drapery, the face of each utterly individual. Like much medieval sculpture these figures were once carefully painted, and they must have been a striking sight when newly completed. Collectively, however, they form a

17, 18

19

20

17. *Madonna and Child. c.* 1400. Paint on panel. The whole 35 × 30¼ in. (89 × 77 cm.). National Gallery, Prague. From the cathedral of St Vitus. Painting and sculpted frame illustrate the extremely elaborate drapery style of the late 14th century, favoured at the Bohemian court.

18. *Madonna and Child. c.* 1400. Limestone, painted. h. 44 in. (112 cm.). National Gallery, Prague. Originally from Cesky Krumlov. Like figure 17, the drapery is elaborately decorative, and in the full-length figure the mannered somewhat wayward grace of the style becomes more obvious.

19. **Claus Sluter.** *Madonna and Child. c.* 1390. Marble. Chapel, Chartreuse de Champmol, Dijon. The elaboration of the drapery makes an interesting contrast to the Krumlov *Madonna* (figure 18). The style is far more vigorous and dramatic and there is an element of psychological involvement between the Mother and the Child which was beyond the intentions of the Bohemian master.

group of impressive gravity in contrast with the hysterical angels above their heads.

It is natural to look for a painter of the same dramatic force as Sluter. Work of a comparable kind certainly exists, but in looking for it, a curious duality in French court art emerges, a duality not unlike that presented by the contrasted styles of Donatello and Ghiberti in Florence. Long tradition appears to have established a taste for elegance and refinement at the French court and a dislike of art which demanded emotional involvement on the part of the spectator. The patronage of Sluter is thus unexpected and, in the absence of surviving evidence, it is impossible to reconstruct the circumstances in which his work caught the fancy of the Burgundian duke. The origins of the equivalent style in painting are clearer and they seem to lie in Italy. An admiration of Italian art may therefore have recommended the style to the French king. For it was Charles V who appears as a donor in one of the chief monuments of the style, an altar frontal of *c.* 1375 known as the *Parement de Narbonne.* Perhaps the most noticeable feature in this painting is the size of the heads of the figures and the expressions conveyed by the deep-set, mournful, eyes. This expressive quality, like some of the compositions, probably stems from Italian painting and, although more at home on a large scale, also had a limited popularity in the medium of manuscript painting. It also appears in one of the few surviving altar panels from the Chartreuse at Dijon, painted probably *c.* 1416 and representing, among other episodes, the martyrdom of St Denis and his companions. Through the manipulation of the facial expressions of the executioner and onlookers, the painter succeeded in conveying something of the horror and shock of the martyrdom. This is one aspect of French court painting *c.* 1400 and led, by devious means, to the emotional expressiveness of Roger van der Weyden.

In general, however, in paintings executed for the French court such extremes seem to have been avoided. Especially in the field of manuscript illumination the most accomplished artists concentrated on the portrayal of detail and on the settings of their scenes without any appeal to the emotions. These artists apparently had an infinite capacity for taking pains over their work, and were given ample opportunities for doing so, since a large work—such as an historiated Bible—might occupy two, or even more, painters for perhaps two or three years. The innovations which are introduced into these manuscripts can generally be traced back to 14th-century Italian painting; in particular the illuminators gradually came to imitate the Italian artists' control of space, which made it possible to incorporate their observation of detail into a convincing whole.

In one field these painters even went beyond any Italian precedent. This was in their observation of landscape and phenomena of nature. Although the exact development of this change is a mystery, it can be seen that in the last decade of the 14th century a royal painter like Melchior Broederlam was still content to use conventional trees and rocks similar to those of earlier Sienese painting. Other artists had already slightly modified these conventions, but no previous development explains the landscape of an artist still only known from his main work, the so-called **13** Boucicaut Master (he produced a Book of Hours for the Maréchal de Boucicaut). During the years 1405–10 this artist rejected the rocky hills of Sienese art in favour of a landscape seen as a gentle, undulating recession glimpsed across a lake. The patterned gold background, usual up to this date, was replaced by a sky whose colour modulations seem to be related to the idea of a misty haze rising off the surface of the lake.

This aspect of the change in style—the more realistic treatment of descriptive detail—did not automatically imply a revolution in taste. It was not necessary to enliven the figures or make the faces expressive after the manner of **21** the *Parement de Narbonne*; it seems that most Parisian illuminators ignored this style, and certainly the figures of the Boucicaut Master have all the remoteness and fastidious elegance of the Parisian tradition. Of all the court artists of this period, however, the most famous are probably the **12** three brothers Limbourg, who worked for the Dukes of Burgundy and Berry and they represent a high point in the manuscript illumination not only of this period but of all time.

ARTISTIC CHANGE IN THE NETHERLANDS

It was at this point, *c.* 1415, that the Parisian court tradition was broken; the immediate signs of the break are to be seen in the fact that the centre of artistic interest shifts from manuscripts and a few panel paintings executed for the French royal family to an ever increasing number of panel paintings painted for far less exalted patrons in the Netherlands. A bourgeois clientele with a taste for panel painting seems to have emerged in circumstances which are extremely obscure. The history of Netherlandish art during the 14th century, as far as can be judged from the surviving works, was undistinguished. The country was divided into a number of separate counties such as Brabant and Artois; and since each had its own comital court, it is to be assumed that the international standards of Paris would, via these local courts, have filtered through to the bourgeoisie of the towns. Indeed, a court artist, such as **14** Melchior Broederlam also had a shop in the town of Ypres, and by these means townsmen were able to aspire to 'court art'. Some sort of civic background is probably essential in order to explain the emergence of two outstanding Flemish painters Jan van Eyck and Robert Campin for neither appears to have begun his career under the immediate influence of Parisian art. Jan van Eyck, although he joined the court of the Duke of Burgundy later in life (*c.* 1425, at which period Philip of Burgundy moved his capital to Flanders), is first mentioned in the service of the Prince **15** Bishop of Liège. Robert Campin was a master at Tournai who never had any documented professional connections

20. **Claus Sluter.** *Base of Calvary group, so-called Puits de Moïse (Well of Moses).* 1395–1406. Chartreuse de Champmol, Dijon. Much of the prevailing interest in realistic detail was present in these figures but now very little of the original gaudy paintwork survives. It was coupled, however, with a distinctive and probably revolutionary drapery style; the figures themselves were set in differing attitudes—never graceful and sometimes awkward.

with any princely court. There must have been a link between their world and that of the Boucicaut Master, but it is not possible now to trace it with any degree of assurance.

In passing, a stylistic change should be noticed as one of the characteristics which marks a difference in paintings executed between 1415 and 1425, for during these years a change occurred in the treatment of drapery. Whereas the Parisian painters produced a drapery style which is refined, elegant and in which the material falls in gentle, delicate folds, this was already changing in the earliest surviving work of Robert Campin (*c.* 1420). It was replaced by a style which was more angular and in which the folds take abrupt unexpected turns and form flat zigzag patterns. The style is far more weighty and the influence of sculpture on painting at this point is possible. Ultimately this convention spread across northern Europe and was imported back into sculpture.

It is easiest to pass to this new style in painting by means of the work of Jan van Eyck who at least began life as a court artist, although that court was a provincial one. Although his later work for the Duke of Burgundy has now all been lost, a votive panel painted for the duke's chancel- **20** lor, Nicolas Rolin, survives and represents the highest level of court art at that time. It is instructive to compare it with an earlier product of the same class such as the Wilton diptych in the National Gallery, London. In both works the outward trappings of material wealth are recorded with meticulous detail and infinite care. But the chancellor Rolin kneels in a marble palace which opens out on to a delectable roof garden. Beyond lies a town, painted with a miniaturist's love of detail. This painting shows that Jan

21. *Parement de Narbonne* (detail). *c.* 1373–8. Paint on silk. Whole 30¾ × 112½ in. (73 × 286 cm.). Louvre, Paris. Said to have come from Narbonne, this silk altar-hanging was certainly produced originally in Paris for the royal family. The unknown master was strongly influenced by Italian art for his compositions, and, although the figures are graceful, their faces portray a feeling and passion not to be found earlier in the 14th century.

22. **Henri Bellechose.** *Crucifixion with the Martyrdom of St Denis* (detail). 1416. Paint on canvas (transferred from panel). Whole 63⅜ × 82⅝ in. (161 × 210 cm.). Louvre, Paris. The new taste for heavily characterised faces made little impression in Paris but some echo of it appears here in a painting executed for the Chartreuse de Champmol. Many of these types are extremely Italianate (14th century). The style by some obscure path reappears in the work of Robert Campin.

van Eyck owed a great deal to the extraordinary achievements of the Parisian miniaturists before him; but his grasp of pictorial structure would equally be unthinkable without a deep understanding of that aspect of Italian art. It was a combination of these two elements that produced a style whose crystal clarity has never been equalled before or since.

The settings of Flemish paintings became with surprising suddenness far more ambitious. This would, however, appear to develop naturally out of the aspirations of earlier manuscript painters. It frequently seems, for instance, as though the Limbourg brothers were trying to adapt to manuscript illumination schemes probably derived from large-scale wall decoration; panel painters at a later date more appropriately also began to think in these inflated terms. Thus a gigantic polyptych, such as the Ghent altarpiece, is gigantic not only in actual size but also in the conception of the scenes. The lower landscape is made to stretch across five panels in a manner reminiscent not of previous panel painting, but of fresco decoration, for instance in the Campo Santo at Pisa.

Jan van Eyck lived much of his life at Bruges. Robert Campin lived at Tournai and it was from his workshop that another great Flemish artist emerged—Roger van der Weyden. Of the two aspects of French court art already described, Robert Campin appears to be closer to that represented by the *Parement de Narbonne* and the painting of the *Martyrdom of St Denis*. Unlike Jan van Eyck, he concerned himself with human emotion and Roger van der Weyden did likewise. Roger's handling of emotion is, however, considerably more sophisticated; and it is indeed

remarkable that he was able to handle emotions such as grief with such reticence that it avoids appearing grotesque.

Roger van der Weyden lived until 1464, and in the course of this long working life his style varied considerably. The importance, for instance, of Italian ideas fluctuated, particularly around 1450 when Roger probably journeyed to Rome. He avoided the detailed brilliance of Jan van Eyck, but developed a range of expressiveness which was considerably greater. It is for this reason that he forms an acceptable complement to van Eyck and the pair are usually regarded as joint founders of what is rather misleadingly called the 'Flemish Renaissance'.

CONCLUSION

These observations help to place in perspective the events in Tuscany. The work of Donatello and Masaccio was not an isolated phenomenon but part of a wider reaction against the 14th-century style which had international implications. The sources used by the great Tuscan artists were not exclusively classical; and, even though scholars' enthusiasm was restricted to the revival of the forms and language of classical literature, the processes of artistic creation did not run along such narrow lines. Artists were caught up in a far more complicated process and their immediate purpose was not the archaeological reconstruction of an antique style.

It is necessary to make these points in order to bring out the peculiar quality of the following phase of Italian art. For at this stage, perhaps for the first time in European history, scholarship really did join hands with artistic creation, with decisive and far-reaching effects.

The Triumph of Antiquity

The title of this chapter is suggested by a phenomenon which became widespread in Italian art during the second half of the 15th century. Artists began to look at the appearance of antique art as a whole and not mainly as an agglomeration of striking or stimulating detail. This development is important since, through a more painstaking attempt to imitate classical art, Italians, artists and patrons alike, were educated to a more sensitive appreciation of classical art; without this, the extremely sophisticated classicism of the High Renaissance would hardly have been possible.

The artistic environment in which this took place did not basically differ greatly from that of the 14th century or indeed from that of the 16th century. Art was always a trade demanding apprenticeship: the young artist, sculptor or painter, spent a number of years in the workshop of an established master, learning the techniques of art and graduating by degrees from the preparation of pigments and cleaning up the workshop to taking part in the workshop commissions. His career was not more likely to be interrupted by external events than the lives of other citizens. Political disaster might induce an artist like Leonardo to flee from Milan (the fall of Ludovico il Moro, 1499) or Michelangelo to flee from Florence (the fall of the Medici, 1494), but most artists like most citizens trimmed their sails to the prevailing winds and continued as best they could. Occasionally external events seem to have affected a painter's whole style; it is recorded that Botticelli was deeply affected by the preaching of the Dominican friar Savonarola, who inveighed against the sins of the Florentines at the time of Charles VIII's invasion of Italy and the expulsion of the Medici from Florence. The painter's acceptance of Savonarola's puritanical doctrines probably accounts for the deep solemnity of his later works, such as the *Pietà* at Munich. But other artists seem to have been entirely unaffected by the most adverse circumstances: for instance, Benvenuto Cellini continued to produce his elegant and decorative works in spite of months spent in the dungeons of the papal prison (1539).

Nevertheless the political and social background to these artistic developments was hardly a settled one. Equilibrium of a sort existed *c.* 1460–90 and it has already been mentioned that to those living in the 16th century this period had the appearance of a kind of Golden Age. Yet, although a few of the smaller princes such as the Gonzaga managed successfully to retain the allegiance of their subjects and the control over their estates, none of the major ruling dynasties survived the entire 15th century. The Medici family under masterly guidance of Cosimo the Elder (d. 1464) maintained its ascendancy over Florence for a time. But all Cosimo's successors were beset with political and financial problems. The famous political *coup* known as the Pazzi conspiracy (1478) came dangerously close to success and Lorenzo the Magnificent only escaped assassination by a hair's breadth. Moreover, in an age of economic recession, his political recovery could not save the finances

23. **Donato Bramante.** *Scene set in antique ruins.* 1481. Engraving. Bramante was the first architect to think of antique architecture in terms of the colossal scale of extant Roman remains. Even in this early engraving, with its erratic archaeological research and its patently 15th-century figures, the gigantic size of Bramante's conception is already striking.

of the Medici bank. By 1494, when his son Piero was driven from Florence, the bank was perilously near ruin.

Other major dynasties suffered from a similar instability. The Papacy was, of course, by its very nature unstable, and the hazards of election certainly affected the development of art in Rome. Milan also suffered a change of dynasty in 1447, when the male line of the Visconti family died out and the condottiere Francesco Sforza seized power (1450). The Sforza family was not itself united and its most magnificent ruler, Ludovico il Moro, was actually for much of his 'rule' regent for an incompetent nephew, Gian Galeazzo: on the death of this nephew in 1494, Ludovico usurped to himself the position that should have gone to an infant son.

It was observed at the beginning that an intense political life is one of the characteristic features of Italy at this period. In the 15th century the political prospect is like a kaleidoscope with frequent rearrangements of alliances to meet changed circumstances. As readers of Machiavelli know, within and without the state no ruler could afford to relax his political vigilance. But the importance of politics for art lies in the nature of the patrons which are brought to the fore. Sometimes particular effects can be demonstrated. The change of dynasty in Milan inaugurated a period of artistic patronage which was more catholic in outlook than that of the Visconti. The Sforza family, particularly the famous Ludovico il Moro, introduced into Milan outsiders like Bramante and Leonardo. Usually the effects are far more difficult to trace; and this must be borne in mind in following the developments which now have to be considered.

FLORENTINE ART AFTER 1430

At the beginning, the development outlined above does not seem to have been a Florentine movement. This is surprising because Florence continued to be a leading centre of humanistic studies and scholarship. She possessed a thriving university with provision for the study of Greek and Latin; and around the family of the Medici, the effective rulers of Florence from *c.* 1430 until 1494, there grew up a circle of scholars and friends known as the 'Platonic Academy', naturally enough devoted to the study of the works of Plato and his followers. This did not, however, exercise an immediate transforming effect on local artists to the extent of compelling them to copy literally whatever antique models they could gain access to. These artists had more than enough to occupy them in assimilating artistic developments of the first thirty years of the century; and what makes Florentine art of the 15th century so vital and interesting is that it was largely stimulated by this living style, and not by the dead hand of classical antiquity. These developments must now be examined.

The influence of Brunelleschi was ubiquitous in Florentine church design during the 15th century. Such churches as were built, like the Badia at Fiesole, or the churches by Giuliano da Sangallo (for instance, Sta Maria degli Carceri at Prato) continued to make their visual impression through large plain rectilinear surfaces articulated by bands of *pietra serena*. Of a development of the more complex spatial aspects of Brunelleschi's late style there is little sign.

In one aspect of architecture, however, the precedent of Brunelleschi's work provided little help. This was in the problem of façade design, for Brunelleschi never built either a secular or ecclesiastical façade (except the little loggia of the Pazzi chapel), although he must have had plans for both his churches of S. Lorenzo and S. Spirito. Indeed, no complete 15th-century Florentine church façade exists. In order to see how architects approached this problem, one has to turn to the façade of Sta Maria *25* Novella—an unsatisfactory procedure, for, like many medieval buildings, this façade incorporates buildings from different dates. Much of the lower part, up to the main

24. Ascribed to **Giovanni Boltraffio.** *Ludovico Sforza (il Moro)* (detail). 1495. Paint on panel. Trivulzio Collection, Milan. Ludovico was one of the most ostentatious of 15th-century princes. The splendour of his court was remarkable, as were the artists whom he patronised. It was he who invited the assistance of Charles VIII of France, precipitating a new series of foreign invasions into Italy which resulted, amongst many calamities, in his own downfall. He died a close prisoner, in the dungeons of Loches castle.

cornice, is 14th-century; the main doorway, the side columns, the cornice and upper part were added by the scholar-architect Leone Battista Alberti in the years following 1456. The result is disjointed because in its proportions Alberti's coloured marble decoration does not harmonise with the earlier scheme. However, in spite of this, the combination of central pediment and boldly used volutes over the side aisles was a striking innovation which was to be very influential in the future.

Alberti also produced one secular façade—that of the Rucellai palace in Florence. Here, certain traditional *26* features were retained—for instance, the mildly rusticated stonework and the round-headed two-light windows. On this scheme were imposed three rows of pilasters, each representing a different classical order. To the modern sightseer, the result may seem flat, unantique and academic; but, distant as this façade may be from the Colosseum in Rome, the fact remains that this was the first time

25. *The façade of Sta Maria Novella*, Florence. Partly 14th-century with additions by Alberti. *c.* 1456–70. Much of the lowest tier of marble arcading is 14th-century, Alberti adding the centre door, the Corinthian columns and the upper parts. Although a system of proportional relationships binds these additions together, the façade lacks cohesion because the verticals in the upper part do not correspond to those of the lower. The heavy side volutes were, however, an important innovation.

26. **Leone Battista Alberti.** *Palazzo Rucellai*, Florence. *c.* 1436. This palace is notable for its system of pilasters, tier above tier, each tier bearing a different order of capital. The flatness of the relief is partially balanced by the heavy cornice, but although revolutionary in its concept the design as such was little imitated by Florentines in the 15th century.

since the decay of Rome that any architect had attempted to reproduce the classical effect of superimposed orders of architecture. Historically, therefore, the Rucellai palace stands out as a supremely important monument in the development of Western architecture.

If the Florentines had been bent on a course of strict classical revival at this time, the Rucellai palace would surely have been immediately copied by architects for their patrons. But no 15th-century Florentine attempted to develop Alberti's scheme, perhaps because of its somewhat academic perfection. Far more popular—because far closer to the Florentine tradition—was a building, almost contemporary in date, by a different architect, Michelozzo. This palace of the Medici family relies for its effect on two features—firstly, the gradations in the degree of rustication in the stonework. There was obvious scope for development in this idea, which must have commended it to architects. Secondly, the Medici palace has an enormous heavy projecting cornice along the top. This feature derived from the Rucellai palace but, emphasised by its isolation, it makes the Medici palace distinctively different from its predecessors. The cornice replaced the projecting roof found on older palaces, the purposes of which was to provide some shade for the windows from the overhead sun. Although not constructed according to strict classical rules, it is classical in detail, and succeeds in lending the whole façade an authentic air of ponderous 'antiquity'. A number of variants of the Medici palace façade appeared during the remaining part of the century of which the Palazzo Strozzi is certainly the most gigantic.

Turning from architecture to painting and sculpture, the historical picture becomes more confused. Painters of course had to evaluate not merely the achievements of

Masaccio but also those of Donatello; and ultimately they had to come to terms with the new scientific theory of perspective construction. This process can be demonstrated in the work of Domenico Veneziano, one of the most able painters of the generation following Masaccio. The Sta Lucia altarpiece which he painted *c.* 1440 tackles and solves many of the main artistic problems posed during the previous twenty years. The traditional form for an altarpiece, a series of separated panels joined together in an elaborate frame, was abandoned during this period in favour of the form found here. The Virgin has been united with her attendant saints who form a group around her —a scheme known as a *sacra conversazione*. Here then is one innovation accepted by Domenico, although in the triple arch across the upper border of the picture he preserved a suggestion of the older form of altarpiece.

But the full subtlety of the Sta Lucia altarpiece lies in the balance struck between the spatial construction of the painting and its surface pattern. In an age in which artists were very concerned to produce an appearance of 'realism', and when a convenient geometrical system for indicating space had just been perfected, it was especially hard to strike this balance. Domenico successfully provided his figures with an accurately delimited space in which to exist; but at several points he placed complicating or ambiguous features which momentarily confuse the spectator's comprehension of this space. The Virgin, for instance, appears to sit in a niche which is certainly some distance behind her. The upper edge of the triple arcade is juxtaposed to the frame of the picture, although it certainly occupies the middle ground of the spatial construction. The longer one looks at this altarpiece, the more ingenious the artist's creation appears. The painting satisfies the demands of reality; but by confusing the eye in this way the painter forces the spectator to 'read' the composition in the first instance as a decorative pattern.

Domenico's style owes a considerable amount to the great Florentine artists. The heavy characterisation of the male faces and the deep folds of drapery are derived from a study of the work of Donatello and Masaccio and obviously differ from the earlier tradition of, for instance, Gentile da Fabriano. Nevertheless, Domenico's painting does not demonstrate an awareness of all Masaccio's achievements. In particular the use made by Masaccio of light and shadow in modelling his figures and compositions was not developed by Domenico, for in the work of the later painter light flickers from surface to surface and in the process of definition line plays an important part. These effects can be observed in the work of other painters, for instance, of Castagno who was a little younger than Domenico. The desire of these artists to indicate weight and volume was accompanied by an unwillingness to reduce the overall brilliance of colour by adopting the heavy shadows of Masaccio.

In this general development the case of Uccello is instructive. He was considerably older than either Domen-

27. **Michelozzo.** *Palazzo Medici-Riccardi*, Florence. *c.* 1444–64. The visual impact of this palace is probably greater than that of figure 26 on account of the greater variation in surface texture. It should be noted that the palace was much enlarged in the 17th century particularly on the side of the Via Largo (right, here). The ground floor was originally open to the street but the openings were walled up in the 16th century, the inserted windows being designed by Michelangelo.

ico or Castagno—older even than Masaccio. He began his training in the workshop of Ghiberti and his earliest known work in the Chiostro Verde of Sta Maria Novella has something of the elegance and detailed portrayal of the International Gothic style. During the succeeding years, however, he became passionately interested in the contemporary discoveries in art. Four heads which he painted round a clockface in Florence cathedral have something of Masaccio's method of modelling in light and shadow, and many of his works demonstrate almost an obsession with the intricacies of perspective construction. But in his later years these interests were modified; and a late work such as the *Night Hunt* (Ashmolean Museum, Oxford) is full of gay colour and elegant little figures.

In spite of the influence of Donatello and Masaccio, a constant undercurrent of restraint and refinement ran through Florentine art which it is perhaps too easy to forget. Donatello seems to have reacted violently against it in his last years (*c.* 1453–66) for he produced a number of works of devastating emotional force and highly unorthodox finish. In a figure such as the *Magdalen* (Florence baptistery) the extraordinary surface quality plays an essential part in conveying an impression of extreme

28. **Masaccio.** *The Tribute Money* (detail). 1427. Fresco. Brancacci chapel, Sta Maria del Carmine, Florence. This detail gives a good impression of Masaccio's technique of modelling faces in light and shadow and his somewhat sombre colouring.

29. **Andrea del Castagno.** *Pippo Spano* (detail). *c.* 1451. Fresco transferred to canvas. Castagno Museum, S. Appolonia, Florence. Part of the decoration of the Villa Volta, Legnaia, and more immediately attractive than the style of Masaccio. Shadow is not used to the same extent and the whole head is crisply linear.

asceticism; but in 15th-century Florence Donatello's aims must have been scarcely comprehensible and still less palatable.

An alternative style always existed. Ghiberti himself lived until 1455 and his bronzework must have been a permanent reminder of the positive qualities attached to grace and technical refinement. It is not difficult in these circumstances to understand the success of Luca della Robbia's development of glazed polychrome terracotta as an artistic medium. Luca's own tasteful and elegant canon of art, as expressed in his Cantoria reliefs (Opera del Duomo, Florence, *c.* 1431–8) may well be contrasted with the unruly vigour of Donatello's *putti*.

Three sculptors, all born *c.* 1430, carried this sculptural tradition to new peaks of excellence. Their names were Antonio Rossellino, Desiderio da Settignano, and Andrea del Verrocchio, and all three were miraculously accomplished craftsmen. The influence of Donatello should not be underestimated, though. These sculptors were constantly employing ideas originating in Donatello's work, but generally emptied of any dramatic or emotional content. The use of low relief is an example. Again, Donatello had continually deployed his figures as if on a stage, half independent of their setting. Donatello's sculpture also

exhibited extremes of human types which led to the intriguing decorative idea of the use of contrasted human types.

Of these three sculptors Desiderio's work probably has the most sensitive surface finish. Both he and Antonio Rossellino developed the conception of the sepulchral monument as a stage on which sculpted figures act out parts. The Rossellino monument to the Cardinal Prince of Portugal (S. Miniato al Monte, Florence) confronts the spectator with a miniature stage complete with proscenium arch and marble curtains. A heavy marble sarcophagus is revealed on which two *putti* and two angels balance in momentarily arrested motion.

Verrocchio, on the other hand, had the most fertile invention. His output, almost entirely in bronze, presents a stream of concentrated and varied invention. Much of the inspiration of his work derives from Donatello and, indeed, seems to have been executed in conscious competition with him. For, like Donatello, he produced a figure of *David*, a dancing *putto* and an equestrian monument. The group of the *Doubting Thomas* was designed for a niche that had held Donatello's figure of *St Louis*; and the scheme of the *Doubting Thomas* group was probably inspired by Donatello's Cavalcanti altar of the Annunciation (Sta Maria

30. **Desiderio da Settignano.** *Angel* (detail). *c.* 1450–1. Marble.
Part of the altar of the Sacrament, S. Lorenzo, Florence.
A major work by one of the most accomplished craftsmen of the
15th century. Few artists have ever equalled the sensitivity
with which Desiderio finished the surface of his marble
sculpture.

Novella). But, in keeping with the general stylistic tendencies of the period, the group is deprived of all emotional
feeling, and the spectator is instead immediately assailed
by the sheer beauty of the cascades of drapery, and the
technical finish of the bronzework.

In painting, too, an alternative style existed. Alongside
the sculpture of Ghiberti and Luca della Robbia should be
placed the painting of Lorenzo Monaco, Masolino, Gentile
da Fabriano and Fra Angelico. It is true that much in
painting was fundamentally altered by the events of the
1420s. Obvious things changed. Houses and palaces were
painted as if built in a Brunelleschian manner. The heads of
Masaccio and Donatello provided a new vocabulary of
facial types, so that the narrow-eyed faces of the previous
century dropped out of use. Figures were placed more
carefully with relation to one another; and architecture
was related more carefully to the size of the figures it was
meant to contain. Yet it was possible to incorporate all
these new features into a work without resorting to shock or
drama. This is the essence of the art of the extremely
26 accomplished painter-friar, Fra Angelico. He was probably
about the same age as Masaccio, but his work is always
colourful, pleasing and reticent. His background detail was
always carefully observed and, like Gentile da Fabriano,

Fra Angelico had a *penchant* for flowers, strange costumes
and rich vestments. But, compared with Gentile, the
structure of his scenes and figures is more logical and
stable, and it is in this respect that the influence of Masaccio
can be most easily perceived.

An impressive synthesis of contemporary styles was
evolved by the painter Filippo Lippi, whose work forms a 27
good introduction to the painting of the second half of the
century. He was born probably *c.* 1406, being closer in age
to Fra Angelico than Castagno or Domenico Veneziano.
He entered the Order of Carmelites (in whose church
stands Masaccio's Brancacci chapel) and to begin with
his figures possessed a heaviness and volume derived from
Masaccio. But already by 1437 this early tendency was
being overlaid by a liking for descriptive detail. A comparison of his Barbadori altarpiece (1437–8) with Domenico Veneziano's near-contemporary Sta Lucia altarpiece 22
reveals clearly the direction in which Filippo Lippi was
moving. Individually his figures are reasonably solid, and
the space in which they stand is defined both behind and in
front; yet the whole balance between structure and decoration, so carefully maintained by Domenico, is weighted
heavily in favour of decoration by Filippo. His painting
lacks the superb clarity of Domenico Veneziano, but is at
the same time more human and less like an intellectual
exercise.

Filippo Lippi's work never has the coldness or austerity
of younger artists such as Castagno or Domenico Veneziano; yet it is more demonstrative than that of Fra
Angelico. And while it has much of Fra Angelico's delicacy,
it can be playful and humorous too. These features emerge
in the frescoes painted by Filippo Lippi for the cathedral
of Prato and in numerous paintings of the *Madonna and* 27
Child. The *Madonna* pictures are often humorous and
the Christ Child is given an extremely unidealised appearance, without having the impassively sour expression of the Child in Masaccio's London *Madonna*. The 6
frescoes contain a considerable array of different human
types and the appropriate scenes contain a well controlled
emotional content. Yet any emotion is balanced both by
the pleasing surroundings and by the delicacy and grace of
the figures.

Painting of this order and quality inevitably exercised a
considerable influence. Fra Filippo's pictures of the
Virgin, for instance, dictated the fashion for the next half-
century and affected sculptors as well as painters. There is
no doubt that his style of narrative fresco also attracted
attention with its judicious balance between dramatic
action and decoration. On succeeding painters, however,
the work of Domenico Veneziano and Castagno must also
have exercised some influence. Unfortunately so much has
been destroyed that this influence is difficult to define. Yet
in the work of a painter such as Domenico Ghirlandaio, the
figures are far more tightly painted than those of Fra
Filippo; moreover, the ambitious spaces that he encloses
are more carefully and convincingly worked out—all of

31. **Antonio Pollaiuolo.** *Battle of Nude Men. c.* 1470. Engraving.
Experimental studies like figure 32 were used to perfect
compositions such as that of this engraving or of the *Martyrdom
of St Sebastian* (plate 30). The tradition was handed on to
Signorelli (figure 46) and ultimately was further transformed
by Michelangelo.

22

which suggests that in planning and technique the style of
the master of the Sta Lucia altarpiece continued to have a
marked importance.

Domenico Ghirlandaio was the most eminent fresco
painter working in Florence between *c.* 1470 and 1490. He
painted two extensive cycles, both commissioned by
leading Florentine families, in the churches of Sta Trinità
and Sta Maria Novella. In both, emphasis was noticeably
placed on setting and incidental detail. Recognisable
portrait figures of members of the two families were introduced into the narrative scenes; recognisable views of
Florence were incorporated into the background. All this
strongly recalls the court art of the years *c.* 1400. There is a
considerable increase in the amount of classical detail
included in his work, if comparison is made with the work
of earlier painters—a feature to which reference will be
made later; there is also clear evidence in his painting of
contact with Flemish art. In 1480, for the church of
Ognissanti, he painted a fresco of *St Jerome in his Study*

which is certainly derived from a painting by van Eyck.
Ghirlandaio's landscape backgrounds and domestic interiors also betray the influence of Flemish painting—an
influence which is already discernible in Florence before
this date. The very 'humanisation' of Filippo Lippi's
Madonnas recalls the development already followed by
Robert Campin. Flemish religious paintings and portraits
were certainly prized by private collectors and connoisseurs
but a few major works were also on public view, such as the
Portinari altarpiece of Hugo van der Goes which was set up
in the church of S. Egidio *c.* 1480.

Sandro Botticelli was almost exactly contemporary with
Domenico Ghirlandaio. Although he was primarily a panel
painter (whereas Ghirlandaio's most important public
works were frescoes), the two artists inevitably have many
points in common. Two *Adoration* paintings will show a
similar taste for colour and costume and antique ruins.
There is, too, a similar treatment of landscape in the new
style learnt from Flanders. But Botticelli's painting has a

28,29

32. **Antonio Pollaiuolo.** *Hercules. c.* 1460. Pen and brown ink. 9¼ × 6½ in. (23·5 × 16·5 cm.). British Museum, London. The beginning of a revolution in the technique and use of drawing. A rapid pen sketch is here used to capture one aspect of a human figure in motion; sketches such as this formed the basis of a new artistic understanding of the human figure.

33. **Leonardo da Vinci.** *Studies for the Adoration of the Magi. c.* 1480. Pen and ink. 10⅝ × 6⅞ in. (27 × 17·4 cm.). Wallraf-Richartz Museum, Cologne. One of the earliest beneficiaries of the experiments of Antonio Pollaiuolo was the young Leonardo. In his hands, drawing became a major tool of exploration of the human figure, architecture, botany, biology and many other subjects.

far more strongly marked linear clarity. His figures have clear meticulously drawn outlines, the internal areas being filled out by delicate modelling. His work in general has a serious, melancholy quality reminiscent of some of Domenico Veneziano's paintings, the feeling sometimes being emphasised by the troubled attitudes of his figures and by the twisting, curving line of his drawing. An artist who inherited this tendency was Filippino Lippi, the illegitimate son of Filippo Lippi, who worked in Botticelli's workshop after the death of Fra Filippo. Filippino's painting is at times barely to be distinguished from that of Botticelli, but he pushed the nervous linear quality of the style to its limits. He conceived his art on a small scale so that even in large frescoes architecture and compositions are broken up by a multitude of small details.

The linear character of painting at this time is very remarkable. At its extremes some works almost seem to have the appearance of a coloured engraving; and this may indeed be connected with the fact that many Florentine painters, including Ghirlandaio and Botticelli, began their careers in the workshops of goldsmiths. Perugino, Leonardo da Vinci and Lorenzo di Credi, all primarily painters, all worked in the shop of the goldsmith Andrea del Verrocchio. This tendency on the part of painters to begin their careers as goldsmiths cannot have been accidental and was almost certainly connected with the training in competent draughtsmanship which was increasingly becoming an essential part of the artist's equipment. Drawing now became increasingly important in the preparation and planning of works presumably because, in the search for 'realism', the preparatory stages themselves became crucial to the success of the finished article. In the execution of large works such as frescoes it now became common to make use of cartoons.

Countless drawings, of course, exist which date from before this period; but the development in Florence was towards a new kind of drawing. A comparison of a drapery study by Pisanello and a drapery study by Leonardo da

34. **Isaia da Pisa.** *Virgin with SS. Peter and Paul.* Perhaps *c.* 1440. Marble. Crypt of St Peter's, Rome. Little is known about Isaia da Pisa but the drapery style of these figures is certainly derived from some antique original. The somewhat pedestrian nature of the carving is, however, typical of much work produced in 15th-century Rome.

Vinci will show that their purpose is fundamentally different. The study by Pisanello will probably do no more than record the surface pattern and detail; but the studies of Leonardo concentrate on the underlying structure rather than the surface adornment. In the Leonardo study drawing has become a vehicle for exploration and experiment; and it is this aspect of the *use* of drawing which for a long time remained unique to Florence.

Antonio Pollaiuolo is representative of this development and was in fact one of the leading Florentine artists of the period. A sculptor, a goldsmith and a painter, his output, although small, contains a precious series of drawings executed in a sensitive linear technique. This was easily manipulated and enabled him with very little trouble to experiment in recording the human figure in a wide variety of poses. Two works survive, each in its own way a *tour de force*, which show the results of these experiments. One is an engraving, a *Battle of Nude Men*, which has an additional interest in that it shows how close is this linear draughtsmanship to the craft of the goldsmith. The second is a painting, the *Martyrdom of St Sebastian*, the most remarkable aspect of which is the way the painter has used the theme to demonstrate his acquired skill in manipulating the human body. Here the art of drawing must have played a large part.

Antonio Pollaiuolo passed on this graphic skill to one artist in particular—Leonardo da Vinci. Although Leonardo never worked under Pollaiuolo, his style of drawing and his attitude to its purpose are so similar to Pollaiuolo's that some sort of relationship must have existed; already

for one of Leonardo's early works, the Scopeto *Adoration of the Magi*, a large number of preliminary studies exist, couched in a comparable linear style.

The spasmodic appearance of antique ruins in the paintings of Ghirlandaio and Botticelli has already been mentioned; and the triumphal arch in Pollaiuolo's *Martyrdom of St Sebastian* will not have escaped notice. These slightly nostalgic fantasies of classical remains are symptomatic of a new development in the attitude of artists and patrons to antique art. Granted the persistent academic enthusiasm for classical literature, already mentioned, it is perhaps surprising that Florentine artists were not more concerned with the exact resurrection of antique style. Very little 'archaeological art' was, it seems, produced; and a sculptor such as Donatello clearly saw antique art as a source of ideas, to be used with extreme freedom and inventiveness. Little by little, however, artists did begin to explore more literally the appearance of antique remains and the means by which they made their own peculiar aesthetic impact. There is little evidence to show how artists came to feel impelled to make these deliberate attempts to recreate antiquity and the appearance of the classical world; for even in Italy at this period almost no artists adequately recorded their intentions. Yet, although this may appear to be a somewhat pedantic aspect of art history, it cannot be ignored. It has already been pointed out that it was through the artist's painstaking imitation of classical art that artists and patrons came to appreciate more completely the qualities inherent in it. Without these attempts to imitate and to emulate, the extremely sophisticated understanding of antique art during the 16th century would hardly have been possible.

It might be expected that Rome would play an important part in this development; but Rome was not an important centre of art during the 15th century. The city was visited fleetingly by a series of important outside artists including Masaccio, Masolino, Gentile da Fabriano, Pisanello, Brunelleschi, Donatello, Alberti, Fra Angelico, Piero della Francesca and others. But the situation in Rome was confused and the ability of the indigenous artists severely limited. There was indeed an obscure artist living in Rome called Isaia da Pisa who made an interesting attempt to imitate antique sculpture; but in general

(Continued on page 65)

21 (opposite). **Leone Battista Alberti.** *Self-portrait.* 1430s. h. 7⅞ in. (20 cm.). Bronze. Samuel H. Kress Collection, National Gallery of Art, Washington. The importance of academic scholarship in creating conditions favourable to the revival of an antique style in art is certain. Alberti was an important figure in this process since, although a scholar and a gentleman, he deigned to participate directly in artistic creation and designed some of the earliest buildings in a consciously revivalistic manner. His own self-portrait therefore opens this section.

22. **Domenico Veneziano.** *The Virgin
and Child with SS. Francis, John the Baptist,
Zenobius and Lucy.* c. 1440. Tempera on
panel. 82¼ × 83⅞ in. (208 × 213 cm.).
Uffizi, Florence. In spite of the example
of Alberti and the presence of other
eminent humanist scholars, the development of Florentine 15th-century art
was seldom guided primarily by a desire
to imitate the antique. The painters,
grappling with the new scientific methods
of perspective construction and the
conflicting styles of art current c. 1420–30,
had other things to think about. This
altarpiece painted for the church of
Sta Lucia dei Magnoli, Florence,
judiciously balances space against
pattern and contains in the triple arcade
an ingenious reminiscence of the now
outmoded form of the polyptych.

23. **Fra Filippo Lippi.** *Annunciation with
Donors.* c. 1455. Tempera on panel.
60¼ × 56¼ in. (153 × 143 cm.). Palazzo
Venezia, Rome. The work of a near-
contemporary of Domenico Veneziano.
Once again, the triple arcade provides a
reminiscence of the old-style polyptych,
one compartment corresponding to each
of the main figurative constituents of the
compositions. It will be apparent how
much more detail is included here, the
result being a curious combination of
marble palace and domestic interior.

24. **Antonio** and **Bernardo Rossellino.**
Tomb of the Cardinal-Prince of Portugal.
1460–6. S. Miniato al Monte, Florence.
Perhaps the most elaborate of surviving
15th-century Florentine tombs, forming
one side of a funerary chapel. Much of the
detail, such as that of the sarcophagus, is
ostentatiously classical. Yet the total
effect has something of the atmosphere of
a carnival float, emphasised by the marble
curtains as if drawn back for a theatrical
production. The carving is of extremely
high quality, and the superb finish,
coupled with the complete lack of
emotional profundity, make this monument typical of its period.

EVOCATVE NOMEN EHM GBG   Q.POTV INSGL   NL

REGIA STIRPS IACOBVS NOMEN LVSITANA PROPAGO
INSIGNIS FORMA SVMMA PVDICITIA
CARDINEVS TITVLVS MORVM NITOR OPTIMA VITA
ISTA FVERE MIHI MORS IVVENEM RAPVIT

25. **Andrea del Verrocchio.** *Christ and the Doubting Thomas.* 1465–83. Bronze. Or S. Michele, Florence. A further example of Florentine sculpture in the third quarter of the 15th century. Verrocchio was a goldsmith by training and every detail of these figures was treated with loving care whether or not it would actually be seen by the spectator. The faces are almost expressionless and the artist, abandoning any attempt to create dramatic interest, lavished all his attention on the lines of the drapery and the detailed treatment of hair and hands. The niche was constructed *c.* 1423 for a figure of St Louis by Donatello.

FLORENTINE FRESCO-PAINTING
AFTER MASACCIO

26. **Fra Angelico.** *Scenes from the Life of St Stephen.* 1447–9. Fresco. Chapel of Nicholas V, Vatican. At the height of his fame Fra Angelico was called to Rome to help in the renovations taking place in the Vatican palace. His style by this date had achieved a curious independence of other Florentine artists. Following perhaps Masaccio, he pruned the detail of his narrative scenes down to the bare essentials. But they are not generally constructed according to Albertian perspective, and the backgrounds and impassive solid figure style seen here probably owe more to Giotto and his immediate followers.

27. **Fra Filippo Lippi.** *The Funeral of St Stephen.* 1452–64. Fresco. Prato cathedral, near Florence. An interesting contrast to Fra Angelico. The church is constructed according to the accepted ideas on perspective, and the whole composition probably owes much to an influential fresco by Masaccio (now destroyed) showing the consecration of the Florentine church of the Carmine. This included flanking groups of spectators, containing (as here) portraits of contemporaries.

54

28. **Domenico Ghirlandaio.** *Adoration
of the Shepherds.* 1485. Tempera on panel.
65¾ × 65¾ in. (167 × 167 cm.).
S. Trinità, Florence. The altarpiece of the
Sassetti chapel, the walls of which were
also frescoed by Ghirlandaio. The
deliberate introduction of classical
objects is obvious, including a sarcophagus
with its beautifully painted inscription.
However these isolated objects are only
part of a very varied setting. The journey
of the Magi (left) is, in feeling, very
similar to the painting of the Limbourg
brothers (plate 12); the background
landscape owes a great deal to Flemish
painting and, indeed, the shepherds
(right) seem to be based on one of the
striking features of the Portinari altarpiece of Hugo van der Goes (which had
lately arrived in Florence).

29. **Sandro Botticelli.** *Adoration of the
Magi. c.* 1475. Tempera on panel.
43¾ × 52¾ in. (111 × 134 cm.). Uffizi,
Florence. Ruins, as a symbol at the
Nativity, represent the crumbling away
of the Synagogue and the Old Dispen-
sation. Here they have been made
deliberately classical and given an
emotive twist through the suggestive
power of weeds and creepers. Nostalgia
for the antique was often a powerful
element in 15th-century Florentine
painting, and Botticelli indeed attempted
to provide a classical garb for such
humanist subjects as *The Birth of Venus* or
The Calumny of Apelles. Here, however, the
participants are in contemporary dress,
many of them being recognisable as
members of the Medici family.

30. **Antonio** and **Piero Pollaiuolo.** *The Martyrdom of St Sebastian.* 1475. Tempera on panel. 114¾ × 79¾ in. (291·5 × 202·5 cm.). National Gallery, London. The comparatively meek figure of the saint is perhaps by Piero. Antonio's excellence as a figure painter, one of his major contributions to Florentine art, is clearly visible in the archers, whose figures seem to be a deliberate demonstration of this skill, but the beauty of his landscape is also inescapable.

31. **Leone Battista Alberti.** *S. Francesco,* Rimini. Generally called, on account of the dynastic purpose of its transformation, the *Tempio Malatesta,* the encasement of this medieval church in a classical skin was begun by Alberti *c.* 1450, but never finished. The impressive features of this exterior are its austerity and the depth of its relief.

32. **Pietro da Milano.** *Triumphal Arch* at the main entrance of the Castello Nuovo, Naples. 1452–66. Designed in honour of King Alphonso of Aragon, this entrance is classical in intention. Little is known about the master-mason, Pietro da Milano, but if he was the designer he had imaginatively grasped two of the ingredients of classical ruins—size and relief. Decorative restraint and proportion eluded him, yet this arch forms an interesting parallel to the work of Alberti.

CLASSICAL REVIVAL AND
MANTUAN PATRONAGE

33. **Andrea Mantegna.** *Parnassus.*
1496–7. Painting on canvas.
63 × 75½ in. (160 × 192 cm.). Louvre,
Paris. One of the mythological works
intended by Isabella d'Este, wife of
Francesco Gonzaga, for her private
apartments. Mantegna accepted the
subject-matter and devised a form of
figure style and dress appropriate to it.
At this time contemporary costume
ceased to be acceptable for scenes derived
from classical sources.

34. **Andrea Mantegna.** *The Triumph of
Caesar* (section four: *The Vase Bearer*).
c. 1490. Painting on canvas. 107 × 112 in.
(271 × 284 cm.). Royal Collection,
Hampton Court. A part of his grandest
surviving work and a vivid evocation of
antique splendour and festivity.
Mantegna's sources have yet to be worked
out in detail, but this sustained fidelity
to the classical past would not have
been possible had not Mantegna been
also part-scholar and part-archaeologist.

35. Piero Bonacolsi (Antico).
Meleager. c. 1510. Bronze, parcel-gilt.
h. 12⅛ in. (31 cm.). Victoria and Albert
Museum, London. Known generally by
the name Antico, this artist's main

occupation is also indicated by it. He
worked for the Mantuan court on the
restoration of ancient bronzes and the
fabrication of new ones in an antique
style. At both producer and consumer

levels, a new intensity of connoisseurship
over the real appearance of antique
figurative art now emerged.

ST SEBASTIAN—MANTUAN AND
FLORENTINE PAINTING AROUND 1470

36. **Andrea Mantegna.** *St Sebastian.*
c. 1470. Tempera on canvas. $101\frac{1}{4} \times 56$ in.
(257 × 142 cm.). Louvre, Paris. This
painting displays an ardent nostalgia for
the antique past. Mantegna's figures also
have a firm sculptural appearance which
suggests a prolonged and detailed study of
classical statuary. Note here the upturned
eyes with their suggestion of classical
pathos, and the strength which the
architecture lends to the figure.

37. **Sandro Botticelli.** *St Sebastian.* 1474.
Tempera on panel. 78 × 34 in.
(198 × 86 cm.). State Museums, Berlin-
Dahlem. Despite the presence of humanist
scholars, Florentine artists were not at
this time orientated towards antiquity.
St Sebastian is shown here as a graceful
youth. Behind is a landscape with a town
of slightly Flemish appearance. The saint
is tied to a tree, not a column. Yet the
simplicity of this painting is one of its main
attractions. In addition, like much
Florentine art of the time, it is emotionally
uncomplicated and demands little of the
spectator beyond enjoyment and
admiration.

CLASSICAL REVIVAL IN URBINO AND MILAN

38. **Piero della Francesca.** *The Flagellation of Christ.*
c. 1455. Tempera on panel. 23¼ × 32 in. (59 × 81·5 cm.).
Ducal Palace, Urbino. The precise meaning of this
work and the significance of the three right-hand figures
have not yet been satisfactorily settled. Piero's interest
in antiquity was probably fostered by his acquaintance
with Alberti, and from this source is derived the
beautifully considered architectural setting. The
fascination of mathematics and geometry are reflected
in the careful proportions and elaborate yet accurate
perspective.

39. **Piero della Francesca.** *Virgin and Saints with
Federigo da Montefeltro. c.* 1470. Tempera on panel.
97½ × 67 in. (248 × 170 cm.). Brera, Milan. Painted
towards the end of Piero's active career, this painting is
more developed than plate 30, notably in its treatment of
light. In the reconciliation of space with pattern, the
construction is comparable to plate 22 by Piero's teacher,
Domenico Veneziano. The conception of a group of
saints in a unified monumental architectural setting
probably appears here for the first time and was to have
important developments in Venice.

40. Attributed to **Vincenzo Foppa.** *Martyrdom of
St Sebastian. c.* 1485. Fresco. 68 × 105½ in. (173 × 268
cm.). Brera, Milan. Probably from a fresco scheme of
1485 formerly in Sta Maria in Brera. Foppa's career is
obscure but he seems to have been deeply influenced by
Mantegna and (less certainly) by Piero della Francesca.
The austere antique character of the architecture is
particularly striking here since Milanese taste generally
demanded something far more decorative.

41. **Donato Bramante.** *Famous Hero.*
c. 1477. Fresco. 50 × 112¼ in.
(127 × 285 cm.). Brera, Milan. The idea
of a decorative scheme based on famous
heroes from the past is an old one. The
novelty of this cycle lay in the antique
subject-matter being set in antique
costume and an antique context. The
influence of Mantegna is very strong and
is certainly responsible for the attempt to
devise a convincing classical impression.

Roman artists were followers rather than pioneers, and most of the notable work done there during the 15th century was by Florentines or artists trained in Florence.

The creative vitality of Florentine art may have hindered any move towards a more literal attempt to recapture the style of antiquity; but elsewhere in Italy a number of artists appear to have adopted an archaeological idiom between 1440 and 1460, and this is one of the most significant trends of what is generally called the Renaissance.

ALBERTI AT RIMINI

One of the earliest monuments in this idiom was the work not of an artist by training but of the scholar-architect
31 Leone Battista Alberti. This was the church of S. Francesco at Rimini which he remodelled as a classical mausoleum for the Malatesta, Lords of Rimini. The project, probably already planned by 1450, is far more convincingly 'antique' than any of Alberti's Florentine projects. This may probably be explained by the existence in Florence of intrusive local factors which complicated Alberti's task—for instance, the difficulty of dealing with the fortress-like walls of a Florentine palace, or the half-finished medieval façade of
25 Sta Maria Novella. These problems did not exist at Rimini, for Alberti's task was to conceal completely the medieval church inside a splendid new classical architectural skin. As a result the architect had naturally a free hand and Alberti was able to create the impression of a truly antique *gravitas*—almost impossible in Florence with its strong tradition of surface decoration in coloured marble. It is true that this impression vanishes within the building where the
35 sculptors Matteo dei Pasti and Agostino di Duccio were commissioned to decorate the now visible medieval church with sculptured reliefs. But even if the total effect is here less convincing the relief style of these sculptures is no less antique in intention than the architecture of Alberti. It is found slightly later on the façade of S. Bernardino, Perugia.

Another project similar in aesthetic intention was the
32 triumphal arch executed at Naples as the main entrance to the Castello Nuovo (designed *c.* 1453). This is a far less meticulous work of scholarship than Alberti's façade at Rimini. It was probably designed by a Pietro da Milano (about whom very little is known) and the sources are as diverse as the standard of sculpture is variable. The sculpture is, in any case, only 'classical' by fits and starts and in the reliefs the figures are mostly shown in contemporary dress. But the bold outlines of the design are clear and the general antique intention makes an interesting parallel to the 'Tempio Malatesta', as Alberti's Rimini church came to be called.

PADUA

For the most remarkable developments in this archaeological idiom, it is necessary to turn north of the Apennines to Padua and to the work of Andrea Mantegna. His appearance is unexpected, for although Padua was an established centre of humanism Mantegna's stylistic antecedents

35. **Agostino di Duccio.** *Virtue. c.* 1457–62. Marble. Detail from façade of S. Bernardino, Perugia. The extreme lowness of the relief of these sculptures is similar to work inside the Tempio Malatesta, Rimini. The style is ultimately based on antique models.

36. **Pisanello.** *Medal of Novello Malatesta, Lord of Cesena. c.* 1445. Diameter 3¼ in. (85 mm.). Museo Nazionale, Florence. The practice of making commemorative portrait medals was revived in the 15th century and one of the most celebrated medallists was Pisanello. The gap between the antique idea and 15th-century practice is well illustrated here; for this medal is excellent in its clarity, but 15th-century in every detail of its appearance. The artist did not emulate the appearance of Roman imperial coins. Novello was a younger half-brother of Sigismondo who commissioned the Tempio Malatesta at Rimini.

36

were late Gothic. North Italian tastes seem to have been conservative, and in this area the style current *c.* 1400 survived with remarkable persistence up to the middle years of the century. The most influential painters had probably been Gentile da Fabriano and Pisanello, each of whom travelled widely in northern Italy and worked in a number of towns including Venice. Both the republic of Venice and the Visconti princes of Milan were well served by native artists, too: and in spite of the appearance of a number of Florentine artists in north Italy in the years before 1440 (for instance, Masolino, Ghiberti, Uccello and Filippo Lippi) their influence seems to have been negligible. Even though Donatello lived in Padua *c.* 1443–53 and produced three major works (the equestrian monument to Gattamelata, the high altar sculpture for the church of S. Antonio, and a crucifix for the same church) it was eventually the native Paduan artist, Mantegna, who decisively altered the course of art north of the Apennines.

Andrea Mantegna was brought up in the household of an artist and connoisseur of the antique, Squarcione. The ability of Squarcione as a creative artist is not clear, but the early influence of these surroundings was of the greatest importance since, from everything that he ever created, it is clear that Mantegna was as nearly in love with the ancient world as any artist could be. He certainly learnt much from the Florentines—probably, for instance, the technique of accurate perspective and foreshortening. He

derived from Donatello various compositional devices, but not the emotional figure style of Donatello's high altar in the church of S. Antonio. His figures demonstrate instead a style learnt not from Donatello, nor from the soft flowing conventions of the Gothic tradition, but from a direct appreciation of solid antique sculpture. It is in this way that the influence of Squarcione's collection of antiques can be understood, although Mantegna's archaeological zeal went far beyond his figure painting. In the frescoes which he painted in the church of the Eremitani at Padua the background is full of evidence of this interest in the classical past, for the detail includes triumphal arches and other classical remains, painted reliefs and friezes, and classical costume. Mantegna had not, it seems, at this date been to Rome where even in ruins classical remains survived in oppressive numbers. These 'stage props' must therefore have been culled from the less abundant remains in northern Italy, from the drawings of other artists or from objects assembled by collectors. The exact source is, for the most part, uncertain; but Mantegna's enthusiasm for the material shines out like a beacon.

37

MANTUA—MANTEGNA AND ALBERTI

In 1460 Mantegna entered the service of the Gonzaga, Lords of Mantua, and became their chief painter. In this position his importance and influence increased very considerably since he had the opportunity of devising a number of large decorative schemes to which his genius was particularly suited. Two of these schemes fortunately survive. The first, the fresco decoration of the so-called *Camera degli Sposi* (a later name) in the Castello at Mantua, seems to resume Mantegna's achievements up to that date (1474). It has the monumental solidity of his early style and a firm grasp of illusionistic effect (probably derived from Florentine artists). There is a vault covered with antique detail but its rather sombre effect is modified by the famous *trompe l'œil* oculus with its gallery of grinning girls. By the **34** time of the second decorative scheme, the *Triumph of Caesar* (*c.* 1486–94), the early stiffness had entirely vanished. The painting no longer gives the impression of a collection of ideas, meticulously assembled, but of a real triumphal procession of living people who happen also to be Romans. The evocation of ancient Rome had never before been carried out with such success.

In the period immediately following the *Triumph of Caesar* Mantegna embarked on a further scheme of decoration, this time for Isabella d'Este, the wife of his master, the Marquess Gonzaga. His task was to paint a series of mytho- **33** logical scenes for the walls of one of Isabella's private rooms, called her *studiolo*. (Various other artists including Perugino and Giovanni Bellini were also asked to contribute paintings.) By this stage the somewhat forbidding remoteness of Mantegna's early style vanishes and his lately acquired freedom in figure painting resulted in some of the most graceful compositions of his career.

The patronage of the Gonzaga family at Mantua is of absorbing interest in the history of Renaissance art. The interaction between the artists and their patrons is unfortunately obscure; but the result of this interaction between the discerning collector and the sensitive artist was that the term 'Renaissance' ceased merely to be appropriate to a purely literary humanistic movement. By 1500 there existed a circle of scholars, patrons and artists with an astonishingly sensitive visual appreciation of the essential character of antique art.

One aspect of this complicated evolution is to be seen in the history of the paintings ordered for Isabella's *studiolo*. This type of commission was new and perhaps oppressively literary in its approach, for the subject matter of the paintings was laid down by Isabella, and represented an erudite assemblage of antique matter. Earlier in the century and elsewhere in Italy it would have been acceptable to clothe the characters taking part in a species of contemporary fancy dress. But now in Mantua new standards were required and Mantegna succeeded in making the antique subject matter look antique.

Another aspect of the same evolution is to be seen in the work of a remarkable bronze sculptor, Piero Bonacolsi, whose nickname 'Antico' gives an indication of the direction of his interests. He was employed by the Gonzaga **35** family in making small bronze statuettes which then entered their collections and were appreciated alongside the genuine antiques.

37. **Andrea Mantegna.** *St Justina* (detail from altarpiece of St Luke). 1453–4. Tempera on panel. Brera, Milan. Mantegna was about twenty-three when he painted the altarpiece and this detail illustrates the cold sculptural clarity of his early style.

38. **Leone Battista Alberti.** *Façade of S. Sebastiano*, Mantua.
c. 1460. The façade was probably intended to be approached by
a broad flight of steps and further vertical pilasters may have
been envisaged. Even in its imperfect state, however,
S. Sebastiano presents an impressive façade.

There is yet another aspect to this 'Mantuan Renaissance' since Mantegna's career overlapped with the late
career of Alberti who, although he died in Rome, spent his
last years in Mantua. It was at Mantua that Alberti
planned and began his two most important buildings, the
churches of S. Sebastiano (*c.* 1470) and S. Andrea (*c.* 1480).
These churches are of the highest significance because at
last Alberti was unhampered by existing buildings or
local architectural prejudices. The more unusual of the
two, S. Sebastiano, was never completed and suffers now
from an erroneous restoration of the façade. But originally
the front was intended to present a scheme of attached
pilasters supporting the pediment and reached by a broad
flight of steps which should have extended across the entire
face. The façade of S. Andrea, on the other hand, returns to
the idea of a triumphal arch. The treatment is very restrained, the main ornament being a ponderous coffered
vault inside the porch which gives a suitable impression of
gravity to the whole design.

The interior and general plan of both these churches are
equally important. S. Sebastiano is built in the shape of a
Greek cross—that is, its four arms are of equal length. This
form of centralised plan increasingly obsessed Renaissance
architects since they knew that its use had ample precedent

in the churches and temples of the Byzantine and Roman
world. Nevertheless it was to the Western tradition that
Alberti returned for the plan of S. Andrea. This has a
normal Latin cross plan with a nave that extends outwards
appreciably further than either the transepts or the choir.
The walls of the nave have an elevation whose elements are
similar to those of the west façade, so that the interior and
the exterior of the building are closely related. The nave
has no upper windows (clerestory) so that the general effect
is dark and ponderous, but this seems to have been inten-
tional, for Alberti is known to have considered an awe-
inspiring gloom to have been suitable for churches; and in
this his architecture presents a striking contrast to Brunelleschi's churches with their brilliant clarity. Alberti poured
the results of a life-time of enquiry into the nature of antique
architecture into these two Mantuan churches; and he
seems to have attempted to recreate something of the grandeur of ancient Rome, perhaps with greater deliberation
than was ever true of Brunelleschi.

It is now possible to realise that archaeological demands
were far less thorough-going in Florence. The treatment of
the subject of St Sebastian, for instance, affords some
interesting comparisons. Early in his career Mantegna
produced a painting of the saint, naked, bound to a

39. Leone Battista Alberti. *Façade of S. Andrea*, Mantua. *c.* 1470. Alberti's greatest architectural undertaking. Like the Tempio Malatesta, the basis of the façade is an antique triumphal arch. But late in life Alberti learnt the value of relief and contrasted textures in architecture. Here the centre of the design is broken into by the heavily coffered archway.

40. Leone Battista Alberti. *Interior of S. Andrea*, Mantua. *c.* 1470. The church was never finished in Alberti's life and consequently much of the interior is of a later date. He certainly envisaged the heavy proportions and the coffered vault, with no window openings. His writings show that he favoured dim religious gloom in churches, unlike Brunelleschi (see plate 8).

Corinthian column and surrounded by classical remains. The painting of St Sebastian naked was not an entirely new idea but at this date it was more common to shew him fully clothed (usually in contemporary garb) and holding an arrow as a symbol of his martyrdom. This shift of interest, which certainly sprang from a renewed interest in antique statuary, was quickly followed elsewhere; and at this point the representation of St Sebastian clothed virtually ceases. Thus in 1474 Botticelli painted a representation similar to Mantegna's. Botticelli however was intent on portraying a graceful idealised human body, and the torso of his saint does not have the sculptural appearance of Mantegna's whose imitation of classical pathos in the face of the figure is also missing. Finally, Botticelli's saint stands in front of a Flemish-style landscape. Neither figure, of course, is 'right' or 'wrong'; but it is Mantegna's painting that has the better claim to the title 'Renaissance', in the sense in which this word is usually understood.

PIERO DELLA FRANCESCA

Mantegna's early style may frequently seem to be reminiscent of the painting of Piero della Francesca. No evidence exists, however, which might determine whether Piero, who was his senior by about twenty years, might have been able to influence him. Piero's own career began in Florence under Domenico Veneziano, and his painting seems always to have retained some of the impassive solidity associated with Domenico's style. Piero was a provincial artist in the sense that he spent much of his life in his home town of Borgo S. Sepolcro where he had considerable local standing. Nevertheless, he executed work for the three Italian courts of Ferrara, Rimini and Urbino, and also paid a visit to the papal court at Rome in 1460. At Rimini he executed fresco work in Alberti's Tempio Malatesta (1451) and presumably at that date struck up an acquaintance with Alberti which was renewed later at the court of Urbino. Piero's interest in classical architecture is obvious from the fastidious detail of his architectural backgrounds. It seems indeed possible that he gave advice in the design of parts of the ducal palace at Urbino. His interests, however, were not primarily archaeological but theoretical (the last years of his life were devoted to a treatise on perspective) and this interest emerges clearly in some of his later work. For instance, an altarpiece of the *Virgin and Saints* (now in the Brera, Milan) has a spatial organisation which, although apparently of transparent simplicity, is of extreme complexity. In many ways this altarpiece is similar to the Sta Lucia altarpiece of Domenico Veneziano, for the

spatial construction is meticulously accurate; but care is taken in the compositional pattern to associate closely and ambiguously objects from various depths in the picture so that the surface composition dominates the painting. The Brera altarpiece has the appearance of a compact organisation of figures and architecture; and it takes a considerable effort of the intellect to work out that the Virgin is not sitting beneath the suspended egg but is a considerable distance in front of it.

Since he worked at Ferrara, Piero certainly influenced the local painters there. The work of Mantegna nevertheless seems to have had even greater influence. Mantegna's distinctive drapery style, his love of imposing architecture and his pronouncedly linear technique seem to have made a deep impression, particularly on Cosmè Tura, the most important court painter. In spite of the strength of this influence, Tura's work is hardly 'classical'. Archaeological truth meant very little to Tura and his Ferrarese patrons, and Tura's style developed into something triumphantly mannered and personal. The strange drapery patterns, the troubled faces of his figures, the startling colours and the fantastic forms given to his architectural features all betray the touch of a brilliant, exotic painter developing his art far beyond his prototypes.

MILAN—BRAMANTE

The influence of Mantegna and Mantuan art are also to be observed in Milan, but again the circumstances of the individual situation have to be considered. Unfortunately

nothing is simple about Milanese art. Ever since the end of the 14th century Milan and Pavia, the two chief cities of the Visconti dukes, had been great consumers of artistic works and had supported artists of many different nationalities. But before 1450 the 'classical revival' and the interests of what is called the Renaissance had hardly penetrated the duchy. Politically and culturally Milan was orientated as much to the north as to the south and indeed, since its Visconti rulers spent much of the first half of the 15th century at war with Florence, the city was automatically sealed off from one influence which might have transformed the work of local artists.

However, in the middle of the century a change of dynasty occurred, the Sforza succeeding the Visconti; and with this political change Florentine artists appeared on the scene. They included Michelozzo, sculptor and architect of the Medici family, and associate of Donatello; Antonio Averlino, called Filarete, sculptor and architect who had visited Rome, and who later in Milan compiled an architectural treatise; and finally (*c.* 1482) Leonardo da Vinci, the pupil of Andrea del Verrocchio. The appearance of these artists had widely varying stylistic effects. The older Milanese artists seem to have ignored them; the younger, particularly the painters, seem gradually to have succumbed, rather unhappily, to the new influences. One interesting example is the artist Foppa, who belonged to the same generation as Mantegna and Cosmè Tura. His early work is executed in the late Gothic tradition of Milan and his late painting (he survived until 1515–16) is in-

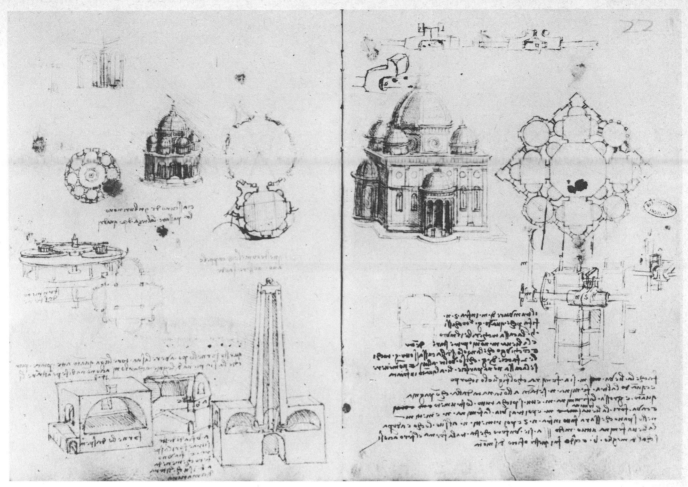

fluenced by the painting of Leonardo. But his 'middle style' does not reflect the work of any of these Florentines. A fragmentary fresco of *St Sebastian*, with its clear plastic figure style and its simple austere antique architecture, brings one back to the work of Mantegna or perhaps Piero. While it appears certain that neither Mantegna nor Piero ever visited Milan, they had a common and illustrious pupil in Bramante, who originated from Urbino and arrived at Milan *c.* 1477.

The influence of Mantegna on Bramante seems clear in two early works. One of these, a series of fragments from a scheme of fresco decoration, is clearly dependent on Mantegna for the linear style of painting and the rather laboured antique accoutrements of the figures. Bramante also evoked an extraordinarily romantic impression of antique grandeur in an engraving of 1481 of a half-ruined classical building, which shows Mantegna's influence even more clearly. Nevertheless, the architecture of this engraving is not, according to strict classical principles, very correct.

After this date Bramante's architecture did in fact rapidly acquire a more authentically antique character. His church of Sta Maria presso S. Satiro, Milan (*c.* 1483–6) seems to owe something to Alberti's church of S. Andrea at Mantua. Here Bramante had to build a church on a restricted site and resorted to creating the illusion of space where none existed. To achieve this, he used the device of an elaborate *trompe l'œil* perspective in the chancel, obviously drawing on knowledge acquired from Alberti or Piero.

Bramante was also concerned in Milan with two small circular buildings—the church of S. Satiro itself and the sacristy to Sta Maria presso S. Satiro. It was mentioned earlier, in connection with Alberti, that centralised buildings had a peculiar fascination for architects at this period; and although elaborate intellectual justifications were put forward for the use of this type of plan, it seems likely that for professional architects it was the aesthetic problem involved that provided the overriding fascination. This problem had already been taken up by Brunelleschi and Alberti and discussed by Filarete in his treatise. It also fascinated Leonardo from whose hand a number of drawings of circular buildings survive from this period. All this interest must have served to stimulate Bramante, and this development reached its culmination in his design for the rebuilding of St Peter's, Rome, in the first decade of the next century.

But the peculiar artistic demands of Milanese taste meant that Bramante, like Michelozzo and Filarete, were each in turn compelled to cover their work in this city with an excessive incrustation of ornament. (This peculiarity of the wealthy citizens and their rulers is best exemplified in their own extraordinary cathedral.) As long as Bramante remained in Milan, his fundamental appreciation of the character of antique architecture tended to be hidden by inessential ornament; and it is one of the stranger features of his career that on arrival in Rome (1499) his style underwent an abrupt change, as though suddenly purged of the excesses of his Milanese creations.

High Renaissance and After

43. **Bertoldo.** *A Battle Scene. c.* 1485. Bronze. 17 × 39 in. (43 × 99 cm.). Museo Nazionale, Florence. For a short time Bertoldo was the master of the young Michelangelo and passed on to him some of his understanding of antique art. Here he recreated an antique relief of a battle scene. The mutilated original is still in Pisa and it seems that Bertoldo supplied from his imagination a large section in the centre which is missing there.

With the turn of the century, Italy once more became a prey to foreign invaders. At first, the country was a battle-ground between the French and Spaniards when Charles VIII of France invaded with the intention of conquering the Kingdom of Naples (then ruled by Spaniards). But by 1520 it became the scene of a far more serious struggle between Francis I of France and the Habsburg emperor Charles V when the French tried to hold on to their existing gains (particularly the duchy of Milan), and the emperor attempted to expel them from their influential position. Eventually the Habsburgs triumphed, and by the Peace of Cambrai (1529) Francis I renounced all his Italian claims, but during the struggle Italy had once more been con-tinuously crossed by foreign armies, Rome had been sacked by mutinous German troops, while Florence had again briefly expelled the Medici family. Such was the unstable political background of the High Renaissance and the beginnings of what has been termed Mannerism in art.

The revival of Rome as a major centre of patronage is one of the most important aspects of the history of Italian art during the period 1450–1550. Politically the 15th-century popes were extremely weak. Nominally they were over-lords of a large area in central Italy stretching from Bologna in the north to Terracina in the south. In practice, however, towns like Bologna, Rimini and Perugia were ruled by the local families and pursued independent poli-cies. The city of Rome was perpetually prey to the disputes of families such as the Orsini and Colonna. Not until the reign of Alexander VI (Rodrigo Borgia, 1492–1503) did any pope seriously undertake the problem of making a reality out of the far-reaching claims of the Papacy to political authority. Pope Alexander attempted to achieve these aims through the activity of his natural son Cesare Borgia, whose meteoric career in subduing the petty tyrants and *condottieri* of central Italy and the Romagna was the subject of classic analysis in Machiavelli's *Prince*. The Borgia plans fell into ruins through the unexpected death of Alexander, but the succeeding pope Julius II pursued similar aims in attempting to make the papal authority both respected and feared, even though as a della Rovere (from Savona, on the Italian Riviera) he was the personal enemy of the Borgias. The troubles of the papacy during the 14th century (first, the Avignonese 'exile' and then the Great Schism) had had disastrous consequences for the production of works of art in Rome. Recovery took a long time. For most of the 15th century the capital of Christianity, although frequently visited by the best artists, was inhabited by none. Roman art remained extraordi-narily provincial, and it was not until the beginning of the 16th century during the political recovery of the Papacy that Rome became once more, as it had been in the 13th century, a permanent centre for the production of the highest quality art.

There are two possible explanations for this slow re-covery. Firstly, there is no doubt that the prevailing system of patronage made it difficult to establish an artistic centre where none already existed. Patrons were jealous of their *protégés* and guarded them carefully. They allowed artists under their patronage to travel, but only on condition that they returned; for instance Lodovico Gonzaga was prepared to send Andrea Mantegna to Rome, but the latter worked there for the pope on the basis of a temporary loan. It must be admitted, too, that the artists often tended to gravitate towards a single court or patron, much as a modern writer may gravitate towards a single publisher.

Secondly, Rome was governed by an institution (the Papacy) rather than a dynasty, and this fact made it more difficult for the city to be a settled centre of patronage. Of course, the succession to the Papacy was frequently influenced by dynastic considerations; but the artists' futures were often insecure in these circumstances, for the projects of one pope might well be abandoned by his successor.

This situation was remedied by a disturbance of the balance of power at the beginning of the 16th century. It happened that the election of Julius II (1503), one of the most militant and forceful popes ever to reign, coincided with a period of grave Florentine political instability and weakness. As the result of a revolution in 1494 the Medici had been expelled (with their supporters) and Florence became briefly and precariously a republic. The leaders of this republic were in no position to resist Pope Julius; and one of the results of this weakness was the departure of a series of artists of major calibre such as Michelangelo, Raphael, Andrea Sansovino and Jacopo Sansovino—all of whom went to Rome to work at the papal court.

By a further stroke of fortune Julius II was succeeded by two members of the Medici family, Leo X (1513–21) and Clement VII (1523–34). The Florentine artists did not therefore all disappear back to Florence since, although the Medici family was restored in Florence (1512), the head of the dynasty was ruler of Rome. These three popes were amongst the most avid patrons of the arts and under their leadership Italian art became centred on Rome in a manner hitherto without parallel. This 'golden age' lasted only until the Sack of Rome in 1527; but it is not fanciful to see in the works of art produced in Rome at this point in history an art which ultimately changed the face of Italy and Europe.

The art produced in Rome during the years up to *c.* 1520 is usually described as the High Renaissance; and while the label has a general convenience, it will be seen that any search for a 'High Renaissance style' has its own dangers. The great artists who worked in Rome during this period were strongly contrasted in temperament and personality (the major contrast was, of course, between Michelangelo and Raphael); and these personal contrasts and antagonisms found artistic expression in contrasted conceptions of painting, sculpture or architecture. It is fruitless for these reasons to search for a uniform High Renaissance style. What emerges is rather a series of new departures in art, each in turn capable of being developed and reinterpreted with great variety by different artists.

44. **Michelangelo.** *Bacchus. c.* 1447. Marble. h. 80 in. (203 cm.). Museo Nazionale, Florence. This figure was carved for Jacopo Galli and it was intended to stand in a garden amongst a collection of antique statuary. The piece is inspired by antiquity but given a personal and to some extent repulsive interpretation which makes it very different from, for instance, the type of classicism favoured by the Lombardi family in Venice (compare figure 88).

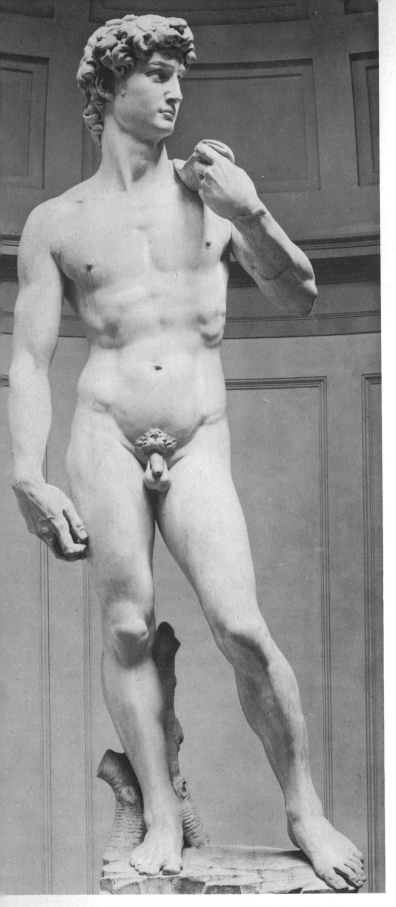

To understand the achievements of these giants of the Renaissance it is necessary to trace their careers before their arrival in Rome and, in particular, to analyse the development of sculpture and painting in Florence *c*. 1500. During the last decade of the 15th century Florentine sculptors appear to have accepted the movement for classical reconstruction in its entirety. Thus Bertoldo, the sculptor of the Medici, reworked the composition of an antique relief 43 as an artistic exercise, supplying from his imagination parts missing in the original. At about the same time the young Michelangelo carved a sleeping *putto* which was mistaken by connoisseurs for an antique; and his execution of a figure of *Bacchus* (now in the Bargello, Florence) shows the 44 extent to which not merely the subject-matter of classical sculptors, but also the style were now taken over. This figure of *Bacchus* has a special interest for the illustration of the character of these developments in Florence; for the model used by Michelangelo—probably a *Bacchus* of Praxiteles—was certainly similar to the model underlying the near-contemporary *Adam* of Tullio Lombardo in New 88 York. It is easy to see how each artist extracted and emphasised completely different characteristics from his model. Tullio emphasised the surface characteristics of Praxiteles' work; but Michelangelo achieved a disturbing flaccid quality in the surface of the flesh and also vigorously reinterpreted the subject-matter itself, producing a figure at once fascinating and repulsive.

Michelangelo's figure of *David* is however undoubtedly 45 the greatest sculptural monument to the 'classical revival' in Florence. This represents the revival of an earlier project (1462), and the marble block which Michelangelo used had already been partially worked by an earlier sculptor. The revival of the project is not surprising since the image of David seems to have exercised a peculiar fascination on the Florentines throughout the 15th century as a symbol of freedom overcoming tyranny (Goliath). Indeed in 1501 the Palazzo della Signoria of Florence already possessed three representations of David (two by Donatello, one by Verrocchio), and the creation of a further figure, of giant stature and destined to stand in the main square, carried with it overtones of political defiance on the part of the new-born republic. But the statue which emerged from Michelangelo's hands was more than this. His gigantic naked male figure successfully challenged comparison with the great naked antique statues of gods and heroes. Thus it was possible for the historian Vasari, looking back from the middle of the century, to say that the *David* had 'stolen the thunder of all statues, whether modern or ancient, Greek or Latin'.

The monumental figure style which characterises all Michelangelo's work (sculpture or painting) can in part be traced back to the use to which he put antique models and to the 'triumph of antiquity' in Florence at this moment.

45. **Michelangelo.** *David*. 1501–4. Marble. h. 16 ft 10½ in. (514 cm.). Accademia, Florence. This is one of the most important statues in the history of the Renaissance. Here for the first time a sculptor successfully emulated both the scale and the physique of the colossal figures of antiquity. The *David* set new standards of public statuary and, looking back from the middle of the 16th century, the historian Vasari could still give it his unstinted praise.

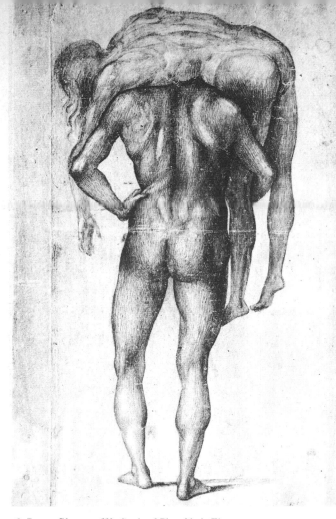

46. **Luca Signorelli.** *Study of Two Nude Figures. c.* 1503. Watercolour, heightened with white. 14 × 10 in. (35·5 × 25·5 cm.). Louvre, Paris. Executed during the period of the Orvieto frescoes, and, indeed, very similar to two figures visible in plate 42. Signorelli was an important precursor of Michelangelo in his interest in the nude form.

47. **Michelangelo.** *The Battle of Cascina* (study). 1504–5. Pen and brush with ink and heightened with white. 28½ × 11½ in. (42 × 29 cm.). British Museum, London. The care with which Michelangelo constructed the fresco of the *Battle of Cascina* is evident from its fragmentary remains in drawings and sketches. This study shows that Michelangelo, being a sculptor, brought to his drawings a far more sensitive appreciation of the surface qualities of the human torso than was ever possessed by predecessors such as Signorelli.

But to execute a single gigantic figure, like the *David*, was one thing: to imagine a world peopled entirely by gigantic monumental beings (as in the Sistine ceiling) was to imagine a new artistic world which could only be conquered by degrees. This development—or for that matter the achievements of Leonardo or Raphael—would not have been possible without the peculiar Florentine developments in the use and technique of drawing, which have already been mentioned in the previous chapter. The mastery of *disegno* came to have an overriding importance in the training of Florentine and Roman artists and sculptors, since *disegno* was regarded as the tool with which artistic ideas were stated and developed, and through which new ideas received experiment.

The importance of Antonio Pollaiuolo (with his influence on Leonardo da Vinci) has already been mentioned. Pollaiuolo had a further, perhaps unexpected follower in Luca Signorelli, an Umbrian artist from Cortona. This was unexpected because Signorelli had been a pupil of Piero della Francesca and, on the face of it, nothing could appear less likely to be successful than an attempt to mingle the heavy, majestic style of Piero with the decorative and vigorous style of Pollaiuolo. But the unexpected happened; and, although in the course of a long career

Signorelli produced a large amount of uninspiring provincial work, he also produced a handful of works of great intrinsic and historical significance.

In particular figure painting seems to gain a new dimension in the fresco cycle in the cathedral of Orvieto. The subject-matter of these frescoes, events leading up to the Last Judgment, was interpreted by Signorelli to allow him to display his ability to manipulate the human figure with the facility of Pollaiuolo and the gravity of Piero. But this singular achievement was not attained without a considerable amount of detailed experiment, the record of which lies in a series of masterly drawings. *Disegno*, once more, was used as a means of exploration.

The extent to which Michelangelo was influenced by Signorelli is difficult to determine, although he almost certainly saw the Orvieto frescoes which were completed between the execution of the *David* and his next great public work, the fresco of the *Battle of Cascina*. This fresco was to have been painted in the Great Hall of the Palazzo Vecchio in Florence, and it depicted a famous Florentine victory. As a battle picture it might have been expected to take its character from the tradition established in Florence by Uccello in such works as the *Battle of S. Romano* (now in the National Gallery, London). Michelangelo chose to

42

46

47

48. *The Battle of Cascina.* Grisaille on panel. 30⅛ × 51⅜ in. (76 × 130 cm.). 16th-century copy after Michelangelo. Collection of the Earl of Leicester, Holkham Hall. The original (1504–5) was intended for the Palazzo Vecchio, Florence, and this copy represents the central group of the composition. It is interesting to compare it with Leonardo's pendant picture (figure 49) since the approach to the treatment of the subject-matter of a battle scene is so different. Michelangelo's interests were closer to those of Signorelli (plate 42).

49. *The Battle of Anghiari.* Free variant by Rubens after Leonardo da Vinci. *c.* 1615. Chalk with pen and gouache. Louvre, Paris. Original (1503–6) intended for the Palazzo Vecchio, Florence. This work, so very different from that of Michelangelo (figure 48), allowed Leonardo to explore further two sets of problems which had already fascinated him—that of conveying human emotion and that of capturing the movement of horses.

show, however, not the battle of Cascina itself but a preliminary episode in which the Florentine troops were caught unawares in a state indicated by the nickname of the composition *The Bathers*. It was at this point that his imagination may have been fired by the example of Signorelli, for he too interpreted his subject-matter to enable him to display his mastery of the human form.

This unconventional treatment of a battle subject must have been the more striking in that, on an adjacent wall, the council set to work Leonardo da Vinci on yet another battle subject, the *Battle of Anghiari*; and Leonardo certainly interpreted the task in the way expected—he showed men fighting—and used the subject-matter to enable him to display two features in which *he* excelled—the portrayal of human emotion and the portrayal of horses. Thus the projected frescoes for the Florentine council chamber presented the inhabitants of Florence with two sharply contrasted artistic experiences. The complicated movement and vivid ferocity of Leonardo's project would probably have made the most immediate impact. Yet no Florentine, looking back, would have been able to find any adequate 15th-century precedent for the precision, weight and monumentality of Michelangelo's nudes. At a single step the young artist progressed far beyond any possible precedents. Nobody before had drawn the human form with such impressive weight and body; equally, nobody had combined the sum of these forms into such a closely knit and balanced surface pattern.

Nevertheless, the importance of Leonardo da Vinci's return to Florence should not be underestimated. For about seventeen years this celebrated genius had been in the service of the Sforza dukes of Milan, for whom he had taken on a number of diverse tasks such as the painting of *The Last Supper* (Sta Maria delle Grazie), or the modelling of a gigantic equestrian monument to Francesco Sforza. The Florentine and Paduan antique revivals seem to have

passed him by; and this, combined with the fact that he belonged to a generation older than that of Michelangelo, probably accounts for his more traditional treatment of the battle theme in the council chamber. But during his absence Leonardo's attitude to light and colour in painting had changed out of all recognition, and his return projected a new style of painting into the artistic world of Florence. He now used delicate and sober colouring; his paintings possessed a sensitive tonal unity; and, by contrast with the brilliant definition of his early painting, the transitions from light to shadow were gently blurred in a technique later called *sfumato* (indicating that the individual degrees of these transitions had 'vanished'). At its most obvious this contrast of styles may be seen by setting the early Uffizi *Annunciation* alongside the Louvre *Virgin and Child with St Anne*.

This picture in the Louvre also demonstrates a further novel aspect of Leonardo's painting. His figure compositions, like this one, immediately attracted attention on account of their fascinating complexity. Soft, gentle and sinuous, this was a style opposed in most particulars to the world of *David* and the *Bathers* cartoon. Paintings of this Leonardesque type were intimate; they possessed delicacy, refinement and sensibility.

Leonardo's compositions seem to have exercised a fascination on the young Raphael who came to Florence at about this time (1504). Raphael had been trained under an eminent provincial master, Perugino, who, like Signorelli, had been a pupil of Piero della Francesca. Perugino's development had, however, been totally different. Having spent a short period working under Verrocchio, he developed an extremely graceful style which retains nothing of Piero's monumentality. On the other hand, Perugino derived from Piero an insight into the underlying geometry of space and proportion and (also probably from Piero) a more sensitive approach to colour. All these things he **44** handed on to his pupil Raphael; and it is not surprising therefore that to Raphael the paintings of Leonardo in their grace and colour must have seemed to explore anew those things in art that he already valued. Raphael certainly reworked and developed a number of Leonardesque schemes during these years; and he was among the first to attempt to emulate Leonardo's complex portrait style.

Shortly before going to Rome Raphael had also begun to experiment with the vigorous figure drawing of the Florentine tradition. This is to be seen in the *Deposition* painted in 1507 for a Perugian patroness, Atlanta Baglioni. This painting has a particular interest because a number of drawings survive which record the evolution of the composition from a static graceful Peruginesque arrangement of figures to the violent and strenuous action seen in the finished painting.

In these works is presented the genesis of those contrasts which mark the mature style of Raphael and Michelangelo in Rome. One general point deserves comment; taken collectively, the works which have been examined present a far greater range of human and emotional expression than is to be found in the previous decades of Florentine art. The generation which produced Andrea del Verrocchio had valued the decorative aspects of art without paying much attention to the emotional content of their subjects, or to the dramatic impact which a work might make on the spectator. The last fifteen years of the century saw a significant swing in Florentine taste. The late *Visitation* of Ghirlandaio is charged with emotional feeling which is not concealed by the superficially decorative character. The painting of Botticelli becomes increasingly troubled and serious in its emotional tone. The solemn character of Michelangelo's early sculpture (the Vatican *Pietà*, for example) is also remarkable; and this solemnity was shared by much of the sculpture of Andrea Sansovino. To these must also be added the subtle sweetness and sentiment of Leonardo's female figures, and the grotesque fury of his battling warriors, so that it can be seen that the rising generation of artists had a major task of assimilation before them. No artist could now easily avoid the problem of endowing any given work with an appropriate emotional tone or a unified dramatic force.

ROMAN ART FROM JULIUS II TO THE SACK OF THE CITY

It was at this point that Pope Julius II began summoning artists to serve him in Rome to further his ambitious schemes for the rebuilding and embellishment of the Vatican palace and basilica. These schemes find their most obvious expression in the architectural projects of Donato Bramante who, it will be remembered, had arrived in Rome in 1499 during the pontificate of Alexander VI (Borgia). Bramante was responsible for such widely differing projects as the Tempietto at S. Pietro in Montorio (1502), the Belvedere court in the Vatican, and the first plans for the complete rebuilding of St Peter's

50. **Leonardo da Vinci.** *Virgin and Child with St Anne. c.* 1500–7. Paint on panel. $67\frac{1}{8} \times 50\frac{7}{8}$ in. (170 × 129 cm.). Louvre, Paris. The origins of this composition date from Leonardo's stay in Milan although the work was chiefly painted in Florence. It has a sinuous complexity which fascinated contemporary artists but the painting is also a study of psychological relationships.

51. **Raphael.** *The Canigiani Sacra Famiglia. c.* 1507. Paint on panel. $51\frac{1}{2} \times 42$ in. (131 × 107 cm.). Alte Pinakothek, Munich. Painted originally for the Florentine Domenico Canigiani. The landscape betrays Raphael's origins in the workshop of Perugino, but the composition presents an obvious instance of the way in which works by Leonardo (e.g. figure 50) inspired young artists to work on similarly compact and complicated figure compositions.

52. **Michelangelo.** *Pietà.* 1498. Marble. h. 69 in. (175 cm.). St Peter's, Rome. One of the few completed works of Michelangelo. It was commissioned by a French cardinal, Jean de Villiers de la Groslaye. The subject was unusual for

An examination of the architecture produced in Rome *c.* 1500–20 will illustrate the contrasted character of much 'High Renaissance' art—a problem that has already been mentioned. The genius of Bramante lay especially in the clarity of his buildings. He had a fine appreciation both of the scale of the antique remains around him and also of the three-dimensional qualities of the components of classical architecture. This, combined with a flair for archaeological reconstruction, emerges clearly in the exterior of a palace built probably for himself but later inhabited by Raphael, and subsequently called the Casa di Raffaello. The positive plasticity of this façade can easily be judged when it is compared with Alberti's Rucellai palace which, by contrast, looks timid and academic. The Casa di Raffaello has extraordinary clarity and a kind of relentless logic which makes it perfect of its kind.

This architectural development was cut short by Bramante's death in 1514 but these few buildings gave architecture, in effect, a new starting point. Bramante's style was certainly criticised—among others by Raphael—on account of its austerity and comparative lack of adornment and decorative invention. These very criticisms, however, indicated a way in which the style might be developed. Raphael himself designed one palace façade, the Palazzo dell'Aquila, in which the component parts of Bramante's design were rearranged and a rich band of stucco decoration was added. This gave the façade a sparkle and richness lacking in the Casa di Raffaello.

This same period also saw two fundamentally contrasted approaches to the use of sculpture on architecture. The

Italy and was treated by Michelangelo with deep solemnity. Here is a new attention to mood and feeling, found also in the work of other artists, and characteristic of a change of emphasis in Florentine art at this time.

contrast is visible in a comparison of the statuesque figures of the Sistine ceiling and the niche figures designed by Raphael for his Chigi chapel in Sta Maria del Popolo. For Michelangelo it was sculpture that gave life and movement to an architectural surface. For Raphael it was merely an adjunct or embellishment to something which already possessed a character and harmony of its own.

It is perhaps the contrast represented by Raphael and Michelangelo which gives to the period of the High Renaissance not a unity but a diversity. The personal antipathy between them is well known. Raphael, by nature sociable and cultured, was able to train and hold a large number of talented pupils and assistants and for this reason his artistic legacy was very considerable, notwithstanding his premature death. Michelangelo, on the other hand, never had the patience to tolerate assistants for long; and, although he aided younger artists who sought his help, he was a much more withdrawn personality. These personal differences were accompanied by different forms of art. On the one hand, the sculptural weight of the figures on the Sistine ceiling may be contrasted to the grace and elegance of Raphael's frescoes in the Vatican *stanze* or in the Villa Farnesina. The deep seriousness and pervasive emotion of all Michelangelo's work are opposed to the more flexible variety of psychological approach in Raphael's; and, finally, the increasing effort needed by Michelangelo to complete any work is strongly contrasted with the apparently effortless completion of innumerable works by Raphael and his studio.

The dazzling fertility of Raphael's mind coupled with his extreme ability as an artist enabled him to master and to develop new ideas with surprising rapidity. One part of this development can be seen in the Vatican *stanze* where, from room to room, the artist progressed towards more ingenious spatial compositions and to more complex figure constructions—a development which accentuates the problem of distilling a 'High Renaissance style'. He and his pupils also devised secular decoration for private houses and villas, such as the Villa Farnesina (built originally for the banker Agostino Chigi who was one of Raphael's most important patrons) with its scenes of gods and goddesses, where a careful and pleasing balance was struck between the demands of reality and the demands of decoration. In another room in the same villa Baldassare Peruzzi, another artist from the circle of Bramante, painted a series of ingenious illusionistic frescoes combining rich colouring with the classical severity of Bramante's architectural style.

The whole decoration of the Villa Farnesina reflects the new 'court style' provided for an educated and critical clientèle. Like much court art, it was a 'connoisseur's style'; but, unlike most previous court art, the type of connoisseurship demanded an academic and literary bias such as had hardly been known before. This does not merely apply to the iconography of these works, although the humanistic content of this type of commission has already been noted in the paintings done for Isabella

53. **Donato Bramante.** *The Tempietto* at S. Pietro in Montorio, Rome. 1502. This, one of Bramante's earliest Roman buildings, was little more than a large monument intended to mark the spot where St Peter was crucified. Both in its centralised plan and in the detail the building has antique prototypes, and it seems certain that the idea of the recreation of an antique building style was foremost in Bramante's mind. Nevertheless, in comparison with the buildings of Milan, the restraint and simplicity of the Tempietto are extremely remarkable. In the use of antique ideas, the Tempietto is an important landmark in the history of Renaissance architecture.

54. **Donato Bramante.** *Casa di Rafaello*, Rome. *c.* 1514. Demolished. Engraving by A. Lafreri. An important building in the history of palace architecture. The heavy columns emphasised the importance of the first floor where the main living apartments were situated. On the ground floor were shops, an idea probably derived from Roman ruins.

55. **Raphael.** *Palazzo dell'Aquila*, Rome. Begun *c.* 1520 but designed earlier. Demolished. Perhaps a considered contrast to the Casa di Rafaello. Certainly the firm structural qualities inherent in that design were abandoned for something far more decorative.

d'Este's *studiolo*. The new style had visible archaeological aspects not only in Bramante's architecture, but in many features of the painting emanating from the circle of Raphael. The 'painted tapestries' which span the vault of the *Sala di Psyche* in the Villa Farnesina would have been appreciated by the connoisseur as a recollection of the awnings used by the Romans to cover open-air theatres; the landscape style of Raphael's pupil Polidoro da Caravaggio would have been recognised as a deliberate emulation of antique painting. And the antique derivation of much of the 'grotesque' decoration, so characteristic of this period, would have been a source of informed comment and pleased recognition.

In spite of Raphael's early death (in 1520) his style lived on in the work of an extremely gifted group of followers who were present in Rome during the early 1520s. They included Giulio Romano (who left for Mantua in 1524), Peruzzi, Pierino del Vaga, Polidoro da Caravaggio and Parmigianino (who only arrived in 1523, some time after Raphael's death). These artists were inspired by common devotion to the cause of beauty, elegance and decorative invention—whether in the extreme elongation of Parmigianino's figures, the façade schemes of Polidoro, or the palace decoration of Pierino del Vaga. All seemed set fair for the development of this brilliant and civilised culture when political fortune once more intervened. Imperial troops descended on the Rome of Clement VII in 1527, the Eternal City was sacked and plundered and the artistic life initiated by Julius II and so carefully nurtured by the two Medici popes was scattered to the four winds.

FLORENTINE ART: 1505–30

After the expulsion of the Medici in 1494 and the execution of Savonarola in 1498 the city of Florence was continued as a republic. The defiant political character of some of the art produced for the republic has already been mentioned —notably Michelangelo's *David* and the two great battle scenes in the Palazzo Vecchio. However, the strength of the republic derived only from the weakness of the Medici; its own weakness was that it depended upon support from France, so that the defeat of France in Italy and the general alliance between the Medici, the Spaniards and Habsburgs led to the downfall of the republic in 1512 and again after a brief revival 1527–30. The Medici family was restored with the blessing of the Emperor Charles V who elevated the city to a duchy (1530). Eventually, the Duchy of Florence was absorbed into a new state, the Grand Duchy of Tuscany, in 1569.

During these early years of the century, Florentine art had pursued a somewhat uneven course. The exodus of important artists during the first decade impoverished the artistic resources of the city and only in the field of painting does a distinguished tradition of 'second-line' artists emerge after the depredations committed by Julius II. If one can imagine Michelangelo, Leonardo and Raphael as exceptional geniuses who lay outside the main stream of Florentine painting, then it is apparent that there was still an extremely competent local tradition of painting stretching in unbroken sequence from Fra Bartolommeo and Albertinelli through Andrea del Sarto to Rosso Fiorentino and Jacopo Pontormo. Florentine painting did not therefore collapse *c.* 1510. The story with sculpture and architecture is very different. No local sculptor was able adequately to continue the standard of excellence established by Michelangelo and Andrea and Jacopo Sansovino. During the 1520s, after Michelangelo had returned to his native city, his chief competitors were Baccio Bandinelli and Francesco da Sangallo, men of extremely uneven ability. The case with architecture is similar. The most distinguished architecture of this period is Michelangelo's Medici chapel and the library in the monastery of S. Lorenzo.

(Continued on page 97)

45
46, 47

A PRECURSOR OF THE HIGH
RENAISSANCE

42. **Luca Signorelli.** *The Damned.*
c. 1503–4. From the frescoes in the
chapel of S. Brizio, Orvieto cathedral.
These frescoes were praised by both
Michelangelo and Vasari for the extraordinary variety achieved by the artist
in the manipulation of the human body.
Trained under Piero della Francesca and
Antonio Pollaiuolo, Signorelli combined
aspects of the work of each, achieving his
results with the aid of a long series of
experimental drawings (see figure 46).

HIGH RENAISSANCE AND AFTER

43. **Maerten van Heemskerck.** *View of the Roman Forum from the Capitol*. Signed and dated 1535. 8½ × 21⅞ in. (21·5 × 55·5 cm.). State Museums, Berlin-Dahlem. Rome of the High Renaissance was still substantially that of the Limbourg brothers (compare plate 1). Crumbling ruins still mouldered away, half concealed by the accumulated debris and rubbish of a thousand years. The attitude to the ruins had, however, changed out of recognition. They were now symbols of a vanished greatness, to be treasured and admired, drawn and redrawn, studied and analysed.

44. **Pietro Perugino.** *Christ's Charge to St Peter*. 1481. From the frescoes in the Sistine chapel, Vatican (see figure 61).

With a background very similar to Signorelli, Perugino nevertheless produced a totally different art. He possessed an interest in spatial relationships derived from Piero della Francesca and a passing interest in antique remains. But above all his figure style is graceful in a manner unlike both Piero and Signorelli. The value set on grace was of great importance in the training of the young Raphael.

RAPHAEL AND THE VATICAN
STANZE

45. **Raphael Sanzio.** *The School of Athens.*
1508–11. l. *c.* 18 ft (584 cm.). Fresco from
the *Stanza della Segnatura*, Vatican. The
accumulated wisdom of the ancient world
is here personified in a vast concourse of

philosophers gathered round the persons
of Plato and Aristotle. Behind rises an
enormous antique structure based partly
on classical ruins and partly on ideas of
Raphael's protector, Bramante.

46. **Raphael.** *The Fire in the Borgo.*
1514–17. l. *c.* 15 ft (457 cm.). Fresco

from the *Stanza dell'Incendio*, Vatican. The
Peruginesque simplicity of the early
Stanza has been eliminated. The figure
style of Michelangelo has clearly made
its mark in the figures on the left; and in
its composition the scene, a miracle
from the time of Leo IV (847), is much
more complicated.

THE TWO POLES OF HIGH
RENAISSANCE FIGURE STYLE

47. Michelangelo Buonarroti. *Jonah.*
1511. Fresco at the western end of the
Sistine chapel, Vatican. Part of the later
work on the Sistine ceiling. The figure of
Jonah, looking up to the scenes of the
creation above, faces the spectator as he
enters the chapel and is probably the most
striking single figure on the ceiling.
Comparison with the work of Signorelli
will show how Michelangelo had in a
short space raised the art of figure painting
to a new plane.

48. Raphael. *The Triumph of Galatea.*
1511. 116¼ × 88½ in. (295 × 225 cm.).
Fresco from the Villa Farnesina, Rome.
The twisting attitude of Galatea is derived
from a lost work of Leonardo da Vinci and
is a reminder of the influence of Leonardo
on the young artist. The lithe grace of
Raphael's painting is here contrasted
with the ponderous grandeur of Michelangelo in order to demonstrate different
aspects of High Renaissance art in Rome
as a prelude to subsequent developments.

49. **Leonardo da Vinci.** *The Virgin of the Rocks*. Finished *c.* 1507. Paint on panel. 74½ × 47¼ in. (189·5 × 120 cm.). National Gallery, London. The history of this work is complicated by the existence of an earlier replica in the Louvre. Their relationship is still disputed but it seems likely that the London version was finished *c.* 1507–8 and therefore represents the last phase of Leonardo's painting style. The carefully modulated lighting, the gentle shadows, the sweetness and grace of the figures are recognisable as traits which made a deep impression on the younger generation of artists.

50. **Raphael.** *The Deposition*. Signed and dated 1507. Paint on panel. 72½ × 69¼ in. (184 × 176 cm.). Borghese Gallery, Rome. Painted as a commemorative work for a Perugian family, it began life as a *Lamentation over the Dead Christ*. Subsequent changes in mood and content probably reflect the influence of the works of Michelangelo and Leonardo on the young artist. The picture certainly contrasts with the series of *Madonna* paintings from this period.

51 (previous pages). **Raphael.** *Ceiling of the Loggia di Psyche.* 1517–18. Fresco. Villa Farnesina, Rome. The original builder of what became the Villa Farnesina was the papal banker, Agostino Chigi, one of Raphael's most important patrons. He employed a number of artists from the circle of

Raphael and Bramante, both here and in the family chapel in Sta Maria del Popolo, Rome. The *Loggia di Psyche* on the ground floor, originally open along one side, formed the entrance to the villa and is decorated with the story of Cupid and Psyche.

52. **Baldassare Peruzzi.** *Sala degli Prospettivi.* 1508–11. Fresco. Villa

Farnesina, Rome. Peruzzi was also an architect and was responsible for the general design of the building. The walls of this room on the first floor are painted to simulate a panoramic view of Rome seen through colonnades. Peruzzi is known to have designed stage scenery, and his mastery of this type of illusionism may be derived from this source.

THE HEIRS TO THE HIGH
RENAISSANCE

53. **Jacopo Pontormo.** *Vertumnus and
Pomona.* 1520–1. Frescoed lunette from the
Villa Medici, Poggio a Caiano. The
general atmosphere of this lunette with
its suggestion of foliage and the open air
may be compared to the *Loggia di Psyche*
(plate 51). The bright cheerful colours
and the contrasted figures were considered
suitable decoration for the informal surroundings of a country retreat. The influence of Michelangelo is clearly felt in
some of the nude figures.

54. **Jacopo Pontormo.** *Pucci altarpiece.*
1518. $84\frac{1}{4} \times 72\frac{3}{4}$ in. (214×185 cm.).
S. Michele Visdomini, Florence. The most
important master of Pontormo was
Andrea del Sarto from whom much of the
pictorial style of this altarpiece derives. It
makes a strong contrast to plate 53 for
here it is the influence of Leonardo which
underlies the whole work. The complicated psychological relationships find for
instance a muted counterpart in the
London *Virgin of the Rocks* (plate 49). The
contrasted styles of High Renaissance
painters were already leading to contrasted developments among their
successors.

55. Antonio Allegri (Correggio).
Danae. 1531. Paint on canvas. $63\frac{1}{2} \times 76$
in. (161×193 cm.). Borghese Gallery,
Rome. From obscure beginnings
Correggio became one of the foremost
mythological and allegorical painters of
northern Italy. The softness of his painting
and his extraordinary ability to capture
the nuances of human expression made
his work famous and much sought after.
This work was probably executed for
Federico Gonzaga, Duke of Mantua.

**56. Francesco Mazzola (Parmigia-
nino).** *La Madonna dal Collo Lungo. c.* 1535.
Oil on panel. 85×52 in. (216×132
cm.). Pitti Palace, Florence. Parmigianino
was a great admirer of the style of
Raphael, producing a delicate attenuated
version of Raphaelesque grace. Post-
Raphael painting frequently seems
contrived and artificial but these were
positive qualities which were admired at
the time. Hence the careful contrasts here
in size and type of figure and the juxta-
position of the rigid columns and the
curving form of the Madonna.

FLORENTINE ART UNDER THE
MEDICI DUKES

57. **Giovanni Bologna.** *Apollo.* 1573–5.
Bronze. h. 34½ in. (88 cm.). Palazzo
Vecchio, Florence. Part of the decoration
of the *Studiolo* of the Duke Francesco
de' Medici, the programme was devised
by the scholar Borghini (1570) and the
artistic supervisor was Giorgio Vasari. The
contribution of Giovanni Bologna presents
a fair sample of the general figure style
of the decoration and of the taste of the
16th-century Medici court.

58. **Agnolo Allori (Bronzino).** *St John the
Baptist.* Probably before 1553. Painting
on panel. 47¼ × 36¼ in. (120 × 92 cm.).
Borghese Gallery, Rome. Bronzino was
court painter to Cosimo, the first Grand
Duke of Tuscany, and produced an easily
recognisable brand of court art of a frozen
passionless elegance which was much to
the taste of Cosimo and his Spanish wife,
Eleanor of Toledo.

59. **Giovanni Bologna.** *Fountain of
Oceanus.* 1567–70. Boboli Gardens,
Florence. Fountains became popular
decorative undertakings during the
second half of the 16th century. They
demanded ingenious iconography as well
as supreme artistic skill in formal composition for their execution, and full
appreciation of them required a sustained
intellectual effort on the part of the
spectator. Here the great bowl represents
the ocean into which the gods of the three
rivers of the Nile, the Ganges and the
Euphrates pour their waters. They are
dominated by a standing figure of
Neptune.

60 (opposite). **Baldassare Peruzzi.** *The Palazzo Massimi alle Colonne* was built during the 1530s to the designs of Peruzzi (see also plate 52). Although ingenious in its plan, the façade presents an essentially flat surface decorated with a variety of motifs in low relief.

61 (opposite). **Michelangelo.** *Palazzo dei Conservatori*, on the Capitol, Rome. Designed by Michelangelo in 1546 but not completed until 1568, after his death. The heavy plasticity of the individual parts forms an obvious contrast to the earlier façade of Peruzzi (plate 60). Michelangelo is in this respect closer to Bramante than to the intervening Roman architects.

Andrea del Sarto was probably the most important painter in Florence during this period. He was only three years younger than Raphael, and his position in Florentine painting is comparable to Raphael's position at Rome. Sarto, too, had the talented pupils already mentioned, and other excellent artists such as Francesco Salviati also passed through his hands. Sarto was also deeply influenced by the work of Leonardo; and, like Raphael, he produced his own synthesis of the style of Leonardo and Michelangelo in so far as he was able to be acquainted with either. The artists Rosso and Pontormo, maturing in the years around 1515, are more complicated painters because their artistic experience was more complicated. The contrasts of style in evidence to a young artist of this time must have been both bewildering and stimulating. The very rich colouring of Sarto was set off against the cooler colours of Leonardo and the brightness of the surviving Quattrocento painters (Botticelli only died in 1510). It has already been suggested that the emotional mood of a painting became more important because of the wide variations visible in contemporary painting. There was the intense emotion of Botticelli's late *Pietàs*, the enigmatic glances of Leonardo's female figures, the distorted fury of his battle scene, the violence of Michelangelo's unfinished *St Matthew* or the urbane world of Raphael's *Madonnas*. Apart from all these stood the cartoon of *The Bathers*, presenting a new vocabulary of expression in the figurative arts.

48

The enormous range of the choice of style open to a young artist intent on experiment is clear, and it is probably this factor which gives the work of an artist such as Pontormo a seemingly erratic course. The variety of his style can be seen in two early works, close in date. The first is an altarpiece painted when Pontormo was 24 for the church of S. Michele Visdomini in 1518. It owes much in its composition to Pontormo's master, Sarto, but into the relief-like composition is worked an exaggerated study of psychological states which leans heavily on the example of Leonardo. In some respects it is too complicated; so much is happening that the spectator's attention would be dispersed if it were not for the rigid formal organisation of the work. This rigidity compensates for the painter's evident intention to extract every ounce of psychological involvement from each one of the actors present.

54

53

The decoration which Pontormo executed at the Medici villa at Poggio a Caiano (1521) stands in complete contrast. All the disturbing Leonardesque psychology and the mysterious *sfumato* were abandoned, for the reason that a different type of commission demanded a different style of

56. **Pontormo.** *Descent from the Cross.* 1526–8. Oil on wood. 123¼ × 75½ in. (313 × 192 cm.). S. Felicità, Florence. Painted for the Capponi chapel in S. Trinità. It is interesting that this should represent virtually the same subject-matter as Raphael's *Deposition* (plate 50) since comparison emphasises an almost obsessive interest in the human figure, developed mainly under the inspiration of Michelangelo. The careful construction of the chain of human elements is matched by the chain of human reaction which binds the figures to each other by glance and gesture, and also includes the spectator.

painting. The work is no less carefully balanced, but the spatial organisation is of an entirely different character suggesting a real world inhabited by three-dimensional people. Unlike the mystery of the Visdomini altarpiece, the ideas are expressed with clarity, informality and humour. Yet another side to Pontormo's versatility is to be seen in the frescoes in the Certosa at Galuzzo (near Florence) with their attenuated figures, and evident borrowings from Dürer engravings. Yet this was the very time that Pontormo came once more under the influence of Michelangelo, being one of the few Florentine artists whom the great man found congenial to him after his return in 1516. Pontormo's career is therefore symptomatic of the state of affairs in Florence in which a talented painter could choose from a wide number of styles and forms of expression in order to suit a particular situation.

A variety of expression similar in kind and greater in extent is also to be found in the work of Rosso Fiorentino. He too began as a pupil of Andrea del Sarto but, on moving to Rome in 1523, he came directly into contact with the decorative tradition of Raphael's followers, an experience which exercised a refining influence on his style. This ultimately bore fruit in France at Fontainebleau, whither Rosso went in 1530 to serve Francis I (see p. 130).

PARMA AND MANTUA

Artistic developments outside Rome, Florence and Venice (see p. 137) have not the same continuity of interest, although the work of isolated painters in different centres has considerable importance. One such artist was Correggio who emerged from the competent but pedestrian background of the current court style around Milan, Mantua and Ferrara. He was born *c.* 1489 (being thus a little younger than Andrea del Sarto and Raphael). Up to *c.* 1520 his work although sensitive has a curiously provincial quality, containing a strange combination of elements derived from Mantegna, Raphael and Leonardo. After this date he seems, dramatically, to have acquired a new grasp of figure construction (perhaps in central Italy) and his ability as a

painter was transformed. In 1520 he began a decorative fresco scheme for the cupola of the church of S. Giovanni in Parma; and this was followed in 1526 by the decoration of the great dome of the cathedral of Parma itself. In both of these schemes he applied a newly acquired Michelangelesque figure style to the difficult problem in dome painting of devising a scheme both aesthetically satisfying and iconographically legible. In Parma cathedral he also managed to bring to the subject, *The Assumption of the Virgin*, an impression of the infinite space of Paradise, of excitement, jubilation and participation in the event portrayed. In this it has been said that he anticipated certain developments of baroque art; and the frescoes of the dome of Parma cathedral certainly constitute an important monument in the history of art and a highly individual creation of the Renaissance.

Correggio's painting on a smaller scale is hardly less remarkable, for the excited emotion of the Parma dome shows only one side of his art. Perhaps because his most immediate models did not include those Florentine masters of emotional involvement, Donatello and Michelangelo, he approached the problem of conveying emotion with a rare delicacy and sensibility. In his hands the individual's

58. **Francesco Xanto Avelli da Rovigo.** *The Triumph of Alcyone.* Signed and dated Urbino 1533. Maiolica dish. Diameter 18⅞ in. (48 cm.). Wallace Collection, London. Italy was famous for its maiolica. The designs are interesting for in general they faithfully reflect contemporary taste, and this artist actually plundered the works of the great in order to supply most of the figures on this dish. They are drawn from engravings after such artists as Raphael, Rosso and Baccio Bandinelli.

57. **Correggio.** *Assumption of the Virgin.* 1526–30. Fresco inside the dome of the cathedral, Parma. Although the figures convey an impression of great excitement and perhaps unruly movement, this dome is most carefully planned so that the main action and the figure of the Virgin are to be clearly seen from the nave. By following the composition the spectator moves by degrees from the natural to the supernatural world, an idea commonly associated more with art of the baroque period.

possession of ecstasy, the expression of joy, desire and love are all treated with an unerring touch. He raised the portrayal of intimate emotional expression to a new level and in this once more his painting looks forward to the achievements of the next century.

In the years around 1530 the towns of Parma and Mantua once again assume a particular interest through the presence there of Parmigianino and Giulio Romano, both of whom had worked in Rome during the 'golden age' before the Sack. It was the painter Parmigianino who developed to its most extreme the languid grace of the Roman 'court style', a type of elegance which through various intermediaries became very popular at the French court. At Mantua the Duke Federigo Gonzaga had already before the Sack succeeded in attracting the services of Raphael's chief assistant who was employed in designing and decorating a new summer retreat on the outskirts of Mantua called the Palazzo del Tè (mainly *c.* 1526–34). This building was to be an informal place of rest and recreation, and it seems to have been ideal for the most extravagant artistic experiments in every medium, in a manner which might have been considered inappropriate in the more formal surroundings of a town palace. The influence both of the

56

architecture, with its contrasted textures in stonework, and of the decorative schemes for the interior was enormous on account of the immense variety of invention displayed there. It was from Mantua that the Bolognese Primaticcio went to the court of King Francis I; and thus the decorative style of Giulio Romano spread to France and came to have consequences of European significance.

ROMAN ART AFTER THE SACK

The terrible Sack of Rome, although it undoubtedly had profound consequences for the papacy, did not permanently disrupt the artistic patronage of the city. Michelangelo who had been in Florence since 1516 was called back to Rome in 1534 by Clement VII; but of the other Roman artists who had been scattered abroad in 1527 only Pierino del Vaga was to return (in 1538–9). Instead there appeared a brilliant group of younger artists, all born *c.* 1510 and many of them trained in Florence (the artistic relationships between Florence and Rome became from now on extremely close). Chief among these artists were Francesco Salviati, Jacopino del Conte and Giorgio Vasari who later compiled the famous series of artists' lives. The style of the first two is to be seen in a small oratory of S. Giovanni Decollato, the fresco decoration of which proceeded intermittently from *c.* 1535 onwards. This style exhibits what the 16th-century Italians called *maniera*. It is dependent on both Raphael and Michelangelo; but the superficial style of Raphael's history painting and the Sistine ceiling have been so far mastered that the effect is one of effortless grace and ease. From the connoisseur's point of view there is much to be admired in these works, both in the variety of pose and gesture, and in the differences in human type. The decorative conceits of the painted architectural framework are attractive and pleasing. But the painters' mastery of all the technical discoveries of the Renaissance triumphed at the expense of other concerns. These paintings are consciously clever and the artists are content to treat all subjects alike with the same superficial emotion.

The painting of this group of artists presents the strongest possible contrast to the late work of Michelangelo who, between 1536 and 1541, was working on the great fresco of the *Last Judgment* in the Sistine chapel. The choice of subject-matter for this fresco was peculiar since it replaced a painting by Perugino of *The Assumption of the Virgin* in whose honour the chapel had been dedicated. Since the Sack of Rome had been widely regarded as a judgment from Heaven, it is certain that there was some association between those terrible events and the *Judgment* scene which Michelangelo was now called upon to paint. The artist gave the scene his own intensely felt interpretations. The total effect is not entirely pessimistic, but it is perhaps significant that Christ turns towards the damned, and that the mouth of Hell yawns immediately over the altar. As in Michelangelo's other figurative works the naked human body is the dominating factor, and the deep emotion of the artist is poured relentlessly into every part of the painting.

60
59

61

59. **Jacopino del Conte.** *The Preaching of St John the Baptist.* 1538. Fresco. S. Giovanni Decollato, Rome. A good example of Roman *maniera* after the Sack. The most obvious debt is to Michelangelo but the artist is able to manipulate a

Michelangelesque figure style to suit his own extremely complicated purposes. The general effect is further confused by the constant contrast of facial types, all of which were intended to add interest and excitement.

When first uncovered, the work was only dimly appreciated: the most common reaction seems to have been to ask whether so many naked figures were suitable for the private chapel of the pope. The problem of whether great works of art transcend the demands of prudery has a familiar ring in our own day; and it is interesting that for some years a battle raged between those who excused Michelangelo's figures on account of the grandeur of their conception, and those who merely saw indecency in the writhing naked forms of both sexes. Eventually the censors won, and the offending parts of the fresco were clothed with drapery.

Michelangelo's style of painting is as much susceptible of analysis as, say, the work of Jacopino del Conte. The Sistine chapel *Last Judgment* is an incredible piece of virtuoso painting displaying a limitless technique in the manipulation of the human form and physiognomy. But the technical mastery is put to the service of the subject and the work has profound feeling and religious conviction. It is of course difficult to define or estimate the degree of emotional content in a work of art, since this always involves a subjective judgment on the part of the spectator.

60. **Francesco Salviati.** *The Visitation.* 1538. Fresco. S. Giovanni Decollato, Rome. In contrast to Jacopino (figure 59), the inspiration of Salviati seems to have been the work of Raphael and his immediate followers (especially Parmigianino). Salviati's figures are appreciably more delicate than those of Jacopino and references to Raphael's tapestry designs appear in the setting.

But it is significant of this period that it was increasingly being asked whether religious art should not be more serious and appropriate in feeling than the decorative professionalism of the generation of Jacopino del Conte allowed. These feelings came to a head at the Council of Trent (1545–63) at which time the Church put forward some general recommendations on the subject of propriety and solemnity in ecclesiastical art. Gradually a reaction was setting in, and in Rome particularly some attempt was made c. 1580 under the leadership of the Jesuits to eradicate from religious art the almost pagan detachment of the *maniera*. However there can be no doubt that many patrons, particularly in the privacy of their own palaces, preferred the detachment of the *maniera*. This aspect of taste is particularly true of Florence in the middle of the century, where the Medici court artist, Bronzino, specialised in paintings of a frigid and passionless perfection.

58, 62

The contrasts inherent in painting of the *maniera* are also to be found in sculpture. The decorative aspects of the work of Salviati and Vasari have their sculptural analogies and it is no accident, for instance, that this was an age of complicated sculptural monuments such as fountains. These large decorative ensembles were ideal ways of displaying technical virtuosity in the handling of stone or bronze. But the public monuments of Michelangelo and Raphael and his followers again presented to these sculptors a fundamental contrast between the languid grace and elegance, and the superhuman force and energy of their respective styles. By far the greatest and most significant synthesis of these is to be found in the work of Giovanni Bologna. It is remarkable that he was not even an Italian but a Fleming (his real name was Jean Boulogne) who came south c. 1554, and eventually settled in Florence. The manner in which he was able to master all facets of the Italian traditions of sculpture is astonishing. Yet he produced all the traditional types of commission from tiny bronzes to large fountains and funerary monuments; and his work conveys by turns, according to Italianate standards, the ideal, the sensuous, the elegant and the passionate. His sculpture, in effect, provides an essential link between the diverse styles of the earlier 16th century and the baroque period.

57

61. *The Sistine chapel*, Rome. Built by Sixtus IV. c. 1475–80. The earliest frescoes (on the side walls) were executed 1481–2 by a group of artists from Florence led by Perugino. The ceiling was decorated by Michelangelo 1508–11 and the painting on the altar-wall was added by him 1536–41. The chapel relies for its effect entirely on the simplicity of its proportions (it is a double cube) and on its painted decoration. Michelangelo's *Last Judgment* immediately draws the spectator into the world of the supernatural (compare figure 57), and it is noteworthy that this association is achieved in part by linking the composition directly to the long horizontal lines of the chapel architecture.

62. **Bronzino.** *Venus, Cupid, Folly and Time. c.* 1545. Paint on panel. 57½ × 45¾ in. (146 × 116 cm.). National Gallery, London. An excellent example of the style of court painting favoured by the Medici. It is brilliant in colouring and detailed technique but otherwise frigid.

Roman architecture after 1530 was again dominated by Michelangelo. Other competent architects existed such as Baldassare Peruzzi, or Antonio da Sangallo the Younger, but the work of neither had the rich plasticity nor such unconventional classical usage as is found in Michelangelo's work. A comparison of two palace façades will emphasise this point and show how in architecture, too, there was a curious duality of approach. The Palazzo Massimi alle Colonne was built after 1530 to Peruzzi's designs. It is an ingenious piece of architecture adapted to fit the curve of the street, and is given an all-over texture of surface rustication interspersed with decorative motifs in shallow relief. Like the Palazzo dell'Aquila, this work has the 16th-century quality of *maniera* and creates a very different impression from the palaces built by Michelangelo and his followers on the Capitol. Although these were built at a considerably later date (after 1546) Michelangelo's approach here to the use of classical features is similar to that found in the Medici chapel and library of S. Lorenzo which are very close in date to the Palazzo Massimi. Michelangelo's approach to an exterior wall surface is far more sculptural, while the individual parts of the architecture are made to recede or to project much more emphatically. Michelangelo also showed a considerable freedom in his

use of classical ideas. Architecture for him was not a set of rules; and classical ideas were merely points of departure which the architect might dispose of or order as he thought fit.

Eventually an intermediate architectural style developed in which certain motifs were either taken over from Michelangelo, or twisted in a manner reminiscent of his style, and this development may be seen in the buildings of Vasari and Vignola. Architectural surfaces were given a limited degree of plasticity, but not enough to create the majestic and overawing impression of Michelangelo's uncompromising style. Michelangelo's plans to complete the central part of the basilica of St Peter's, the direction of which was handed over to him in 1547, bear out this opinion; and it is to be suspected that he was the only architect capable of thinking in architectural terms which were emphatic enough to match the scale of the building projected by his old rival Bramante.

MANNERISM

Two particular problems emerge from the study of art in 16th-century Italy. The first concerns the nature of Mannerism. The second concerns the improved status of artists and of the arts in general. The conception of

63. *Palazzo Farnese*, Rome. Begun *c.* 1513 by Antonio da Sangallo the Younger. Basically this façade is Florentine in type and would in normal circumstances have been remarkable chiefly for its size. Its building history was, however, protracted and after Sangallo's death (1540) Pope Paul III commissioned Michelangelo to complete it. His contribution included the design of the cornice and top storey, and also the large window over the main entrance. Here the centre is emphasised in an unusual way by omitting the pediment and recessing the window. Instead of the pediment, Michelangelo installed the large shield bearing the Farnese arms surrounded by a splendid cartouche.

'Mannerism' is almost inseparable from that of 'High Renaissance' art implying, as it does, a kind of Hegelian antithesis to a presupposed thesis of stylistic taste. The illusory nature of the artistic unity of the High Renaissance period has already been mentioned, and this in itself complicates any attempt to define mannerist features. Nevertheless much of the strongly individual art of the decades following *c.* 1520 has been seen as a deliberate reaction against artistic works which preceded it. Analyses of the nature and causes of this reaction vary. Sometimes it is attributed to the 'inner tension' of the artists or to the 'unstable complexion of [their] moral world'. Sometimes Mannerism is shown as a species of 'angry young man' movement, and sometimes as a way of life in which 'it was impossible to retain an everyday commonplace outlook on things and the surrounding world'. Mannerist tendencies are seen equally in the confident boasting of Cellini's autobiography or the morbid introspection of Pontormo's diary. At its widest and least useful Mannerism is equated with anything fanciful, extravagant, unexpected or odd.

The term from which the word derives has already been mentioned—*maniera*—which means 'style' and could imply 'stylishness' with associations of grace, refinement and facility. *Bella maniera* was first applied in this sense to the style of art produced by Raphael and his followers; the concept of *maniera* thus began life in considerably reduced circumstances, although later the concept was extended to include all those artists of the years following *c.* 1520. This means, however, that there was no conscious 'mannerist movement' in the 16th century in the sense of a Salon des Indépendants or a Pre-Raphaelite Brotherhood in the 19th century.

By common consent Mannerism is also used to describe the multiplicity of artistic means by which the extraordinary creations of the period 1500–20 were assimilated and developed during the subsequent years; and provided there is general agreement about the *type* of art covered, then this notion has a certain utility. However, since Mannerism is unfortunately fraught with the neurotic psychological overtones mentioned above, the use of the word can become a positive barrier to understanding works of art produced during the period except in a negative fashion. Mannerism will stand not for a style of art of great inventive richness, but for a contagious psychological condition of protest. This approach is not very stimulating, for continually to isolate 'anti-High Renaissance' tendencies is akin to describing 15th-century Florentine art in terms of 'anti-Gothic' tendencies. Thus earlier in this chapter an attempt was made to describe the work of Pontormo, one of the leading examples of a mannerist painter, in the positive terms of a maturing artist consciously varying his style, not in moments of crisis or instability, but to suit a particular commission.

ART HISTORY AND CRITICISM

Nevertheless, the personal instability of some mannerist artists rests on recorded fact. Some 16th-century artists were strange people with unusual and sometimes morbid interests. Pontormo by the age of 51 did become emotionally unstable and this is revealed in his diary (1555–6). According to the account of Vasari, Parmigianino gave up painting at the end of his short life and, 'bearded, long-haired and neglected', took to alchemy. However, these and other anecdotes, far from indicating a general *malaise* (there were plenty of contemporary artists who appear to have been quite normal) are part of a general change in the attitude to art and artists. The causes of this change go back to the literary humanism of the previous century and the evaluation of such treatises as those of Pliny and Vitruvius. The existence of these works lifted the visual arts into the realm of scholarship and gave them a prestige never enjoyed before. Scholars and other articulate members of society took an interest in them and were willing (in imitation of Pliny) to collect and record stories about the artists. This development reached a 16th-century climax in the *Lives* compiled by Vasari, the first serious essay in the history of Western art. In the 15th century Ghiberti, in imitation of antique precedent, had written three *Commentarii* which included memoirs of his own life;

64. *St Peter's*, Rome. On the death of Antonio da Sangallo, Michelangelo took over the direction of work on St Peter's (1547). At this date the central crossing arches had been erected so that the general scale of the building was determined but neither its final plan nor the shape of the dome. Michelangelo's design for the dome matched Bramante's original scale of building and is notable for the enormous weight of the projecting columns buttressing the drum and the heavy ribs on the dome itself. It was probably designed and partially built *c.* 1561-4 but the completion *c.* 1585-90 came long after Michelangelo's death.

and, since memoir-writing is a form of self-expression, it is not surprising that other artists took up the idea. Of all these, the most famous reminiscences are those of Cellini, vividly revealing, as they do, the character of the writer and the circumstances in which he lived.

Yet the existence of these literary effusions, while they shed light on the character of specific artists, does not provide grounds for supposing that the 16th-century artist as a creature was noticeably different from his 15th-century counterpart; and there is still room to doubt whether professional life for the majority of artists changed particularly in the 16th century. But one aspect of professional existence had materially altered, for new possibilities existed for advancement, and also a new type of recognition. The immense prestige enjoyed by Michelangelo opened up unprecedented possibilities for the aspiring

artist. This prestige did not prevent Michelangelo being ordered by successive popes from project to project like a superior servant; but it did mean that his greatness was acknowledged as greatness during his lifetime by an increasing band of *litterati* and *cognoscenti* who were prepared to publicise their opinions. For considered art criticism was one of the most important developments of the 16th century; and, while this might be a questionable asset for the artist, it did open up the possibility of a new sort of fame. Moreover, if artists were willing to don the aspect of a courtier, then the example of Raphael was before them, who rose so high in the esteem of Leo X that it was rumoured (quite wrongly) that the pope had offered to make him a cardinal. Thus in these respects the 16th century was perhaps a century not so much of absolute change as of new horizons.

The Italian Renaissance and Art beyond the Alps

65. **Jean Goujon.** *Gallery supported by caryatids.* 1550–1. In the ground floor *Salle* of Lescot's wing in the Louvre, Paris. In the spread of classicising standards and taste outside Italy, the court of France played an especially important part. These figures form part of the interior decoration of the new wing of the Louvre, built after 1546.

The political history of the northern European states during this period is too complicated to be easily summarised, but it is necessary to notice the recovery of France under Louis XI (1461–83), the unexpected rise to power of the Habsburgs through a series of fortunate marriages, and finally the European struggle between the same Habsburgs and the French kings, a struggle which was fought out partly in Italy and partly in the North where it was brought to an end in 1558. At the same time the political situation was greatly complicated in the early 16th century by religious disorders in Germany and Switzerland; by serious revolts (on both the intellectual and political planes) against the ecclesiastical hierarchy, the authority of the pope and the temporal régimes which supported the papacy; and after 1517 by the swift spread of the 'protestant' doctrines of Luther and Calvin.

The interrelation between political events and the spread of classical learning and ideas is obscure. In 1500 Germany already possessed great scholars such as Reuchlin (1455–1522), who had studied in Italy; but the greatest figure in the 'rebirth' of classical thought and literature in northern Europe was undoubtedly the Dutch scholar Erasmus of Rotterdam (*c.* 1469–1536) whose printed editions of classical texts seem to have made the writings of antique authors available to northerners. As in Italy the prestige attached to classical scholarship was gradually accompanied by a new reverence for classical works of art, and then for the 'classicising' art of contemporary Italy, but this was more halting, and less consistent, than in Italy.

Italian standards and Italian taste gradually came to be accepted as the dominating influence in European art. The crucial word here is 'dominating' for northerners had at no point in medieval history been insensitive to Italian artistic ideas. Indeed, the adaptation by northern artists of Italian ideas to local needs is a constant feature of medieval art. Yet, however important Italy may have been as a source of inspiration, the ideas were almost always converted into the local idiom and to any Italian might well have been unrecognisable as of Italian origin. The development now to be examined has its logical sequel in the 17th century and cannot be pursued here to its conclusion. Yet it requires only a short study of the early 17th century to see that by this date Italian influence in the arts at least superficially, had a destructive effect on local traditions, to an extent previously unknown. By contrasting the painting of Rubens with that of Gerard David, or the Whitehall Banqueting House of Charles I with the Hampton Court Banqueting Hall of Henry VIII, or late 16th-century German sculpture with the tradition of Stoss and Riemenschneider, it can be seen that northern art had been altered almost out of recognition. Italy, from being merely a fruitful but occasional hunting-ground for ideas, had come to have on artists and patrons alike an hypnotic effect of unprecedented strength.

Armed with this foreknowledge, it is perhaps tempting to approach art beyond the Alps with a sense of expectancy, waiting for these changes to take place. Yet such an attitude entails missing much that is rewarding in a century that

66. **Dirck Bouts.** *The Justice of the Emperor Otto : Ordeal by Fire.*
c. 1475. Paint on panel. 127½ × 71½ in. (324 × 182 cm.).
Musées Royaux des Beaux-Arts, Brussels. Bouts' grasp of spatial
effects in painting was remarkable, but his scenes tend to be
impassive and the action congealed. In this feature, he forms an
obvious contrast to his great predecessor Roger van der Weyden.

produced painters such as Hugo van der Goes, sculptors **63**
like Gerhaert and Stoss, or such remarkable buildings as *71,73*
the chapel of King's College at Cambridge. And while it is **68**
impossible in a short space to do justice to these artists and
their works, an appreciation of *Italian* art is greatly enhanced by some knowledge of the traditions which it
ultimately vanquished.

FLEMISH PAINTING IN THE LATER 15TH CENTURY

The achievements of Jan van Eyck and Roger van der
Weyden (see pp. 38–9) placed a considerable burden on
their successors. The full exploitation of the achievements
was beyond the scope of any single master, although a
number of lesser painters developed different aspects. Of
the immediate successors, Petrus Christus of Bruges, an
associate of Jan van Eyck, was the only painter to concentrate wholly and with some degree of success on con-
tinuing the tradition of minute observation and brilliant
detail established by the master. Dirck Bouts, a painter of *66*
Louvain, made a positive contribution to Flemish art in his
carefully organised backgrounds and landscapes. He seems
purposely to have avoided the expressive emotion of
Roger's work, and the action of his paintings tends to
appear frozen and congealed into immobility. A remarkable synthesis of all these painters is to be seen in the work
of Hans Memlinc who worked at Bruges and seems to have
drawn on the impassive style of Bouts, the compositional
harmony of Roger and also, in his brilliant flashes of
detailed observation, on the style of van Eyck.

But of all these Flemish painters in the second half of the
century only one master emerged who appears truly to
have stood out from this general development. This painter,
Hugo van der Goes, lived much of his life at Ghent although *63*
some time before his death he entered a religious house
near Brussels. Since he was alleged, according to a contemporary account, to have become mentally unstable at
the end of his life (1481–2) there is strong inducement (as
with Pontormo, already mentioned) to romanticise his life
on this basis. But he appears to have been a successful
professional painter who, without holding court office,
nevertheless executed work for the ducal court of Burgundy.
The peculiar forcefulness of his paintings is easily appreciated when they are set alongside those of his contemporaries. He was one of the very few Flemish 15th-century
artists whose paintings do not have a uniformly high viewpoint. The heads of the main figures are, as a rule, painted
as if slightly above the head of the spectator who is therefore, subjectively, dominated by them. Apart from this
there are also changes of viewpoint, and juxtapositions of
figures and objects contrasted in scale, which give Hugo's
large work an uneasy and unsettled appearance. His
painting is generally intensely serious in expression.

There were two other painters of exceptional individu-
ality—and both from the northern counties; one was
Geertgen tot Sint Jans, of Haarlem in the county of
Holland, the other Hieronymus Bosch, of 's Hertogenbosch

67. **Hieronymus Bosch.** *The Temptation of St Anthony.*
c. 1500–10. Paint on panel. 51¾ × 46¾ in. (132 × 119 cm.).
Museu Nacional de Arte Antiga, Lisbon. The meaning of
Bosch's paintings is now obscure; perhaps it was forgotten
almost as soon as the painter had died. What can now be
admired are the great breadth of vision and technical skill.

68. *A Miracle of the Virgin. c.* 1480. Detail from the wall paintings
in the chapel of Eton College. The interest of these works lies
partly in the way they illustrate the spread of a Flemish style
outside Flanders. The painter's name is unknown but he seems
to have been acquainted with the art of Bruges and Louvain.

in the county of Brabant. By the standards of Bruges and
Brussels both would have been judged provincial. But the
paintings of each are very unusual and unexpected, and
any mention of their work here significantly enlarges an
appreciation of the range of northern painting.

About Geertgen very little is known, although a later
writer recorded that he died at the age of 28 in about 1490.
In this short life he displayed a remarkable feeling for landscape painting and produced one study in tonal effects
which seems to be entirely revolutionary. This is the
Nativity painting now in London in which the lighting is **71**
derived exclusively from sources within the picture, so that
the whole painting is worked out not in terms of colour but
of light and shadow.

The career of Hieronymus Bosch, like that of Geertgen, **67**
is obscure, and in spite of the fame of his paintings their
precise meaning is still elusive. It is not entirely certain for
whom these works were originally intended, although
later, in the 16th century, Bosch's work was much admired
by King Philip II of Spain. For this reason it seems unlikely that the fantasies which flowed from his brush were
subversive or heretical (as is sometimes suggested), and
more likely that his paintings embroider, with a wealth of
detail drawn from obscure local lore, general 15th-century
moral themes such as the mortality of man. Certainly he
put the achievements of previous Flemish painters to a very
personal use but there is no doubt about the quality of his
painting. If the strange iconography of his work can temporarily be disregarded, the extreme beauty and limitless
scale of his landscape painting is apparent.

THE SPREADING INFLUENCE OF NETHERLANDISH PAINTING

Gradually, the general style of Flemish painting spread to
most areas in Europe north of the Alps. By 1475 it had a
transforming influence comparable to that of Italian art at
a later date, becoming a new species of 'international court
style' in the sense that few northern courts escaped its
influence. In England the most impressive surviving monument to the ubiquity of this style is the wall decorations **68**
devised in 1480 for the chapel of the royal foundation of
Eton College, which were probably painted by a Fleming.
The popularity of this type of painting is also clear in Spain
and Portugal, where a 'Flemish' style succeeded a pre-
dominantly 'Italianate' style of the 14th century.

The spread of this style in the area now covered by
modern Germany is more complicated, and in many ways
more interesting. One of the more problematical masters
was Lukas Moser. He may have worked in and around Ulm
and been a contemporary of Robert Campin, but his only
certain work is an altarpiece painted for Tiefenbronn **69**
(Württemberg). This altarpiece is dated 1431 and thus
antedates even the completion of the Ghent altarpiece by
Jan van Eyck. Moser approached his subject on a scale as
large as that of van Eyck. When the two wings of the altarpiece are closed, so that Moser's painting is visible, it will be

seen that the whole exposed area is treated as a unity with landscape and architecture extending across from one panel to the next. Moser's painting includes a brilliant description of a stretch of water with light reflecting off it. But, although this use of light is reminiscent of the style of Jan van Eyck, it is not certain whether there were any links between the two painters. No German painter ever acquired the complete assurance and clarity of Jan van Eyck, but several artists attempted to imitate his use of light, so that during the 1430s and 1440s a series of painters appeared whose work has a hard, brittle appearance. Such a painter was Konrad Witz of Basle, almost exactly contemporary with Jan van Eyck. Another similar artist was Hans Multscher who worked both as a sculptor and a painter in and around Ulm. Further afield should be included the Master of the Aix *Annunciation*, a work datable 1442.

A more balanced assimilation of the Flemish style took place in the second half of the century based on a general synthesis of Roger van der Weyden and Dirck Bouts. This may be followed in the work of such artists as Schongauer at Colmar, Pleydenwurff at Nürnberg and a variety of anonymous artists in Cologne. Since artists such as Pleydenwurff often travelled (Pleydenwurff visited Prague and Breslau) this generation of artists both assimilated and spread this style.

MICHAEL PACHER

65 These painters appear to have derived their style in general from Flanders. Michael Pacher, a contemporary of Schongauer, was very different. Born *c.* 1435 in the Tyrol at Brunico, he was within a comparatively short distance of northern Italy and the Veneto. From Pacher's paintings it is generally inferred that he visited Padua at some date 66 *c.* 1470. For, in his great altarpiece at St Wolfgang the definition of space became an overriding consideration for the artist; and his figure style acquired something of Mantegna's dry linear appearance. Whether Pacher also saw the work of Antonello da Messina at Venice (1475–6; see p. 140) is less certain, but his paintings certainly contain areas of brilliantly illuminated detail reminiscent of the Eyckian tradition to which Antonello belonged. Since Pacher was also a skilled sculptor, and would have habitually thought out his works in three-dimensional terms, his enthusiasm for Italianate perspective can be understood. It is true that this painting is un-Italianate in many other details. Buildings continue to be Gothic in style, and the drapery of his figures still has the crumpled folds of the Campin tradition.

In other respects, however, it is profoundly Italianate in intention with its crude foreshortening and harsh definition; and it begins to be doubtful whether Pacher was accomplishing yet another transformation of the Gothic style by means of elements drawn from Italian art or whether this was at last the beginning of the downward slope for the whole northern tradition.

69. **Lukas Moser.** *The Tiefenbronn altarpiece.* 1431. 118⅛ × 78¾ in. (300 × 200 cm.). Parish church, Tiefenbronn. The outside of the wings of this altar, when closed, show scenes from the life of St Mary Magdalen. The way in which the panorama spreads across the wings is reminiscent of the contemporary Ghent altarpiece by the van Eyck brothers. Note the skill with which the surface of the water is painted.

GERMAN 15TH-CENTURY SCULPTURE

Both Hans Multscher and Michael Pacher were sculptors as well as painters. This serves as a reminder that any account of German 15th-century art must extend far beyond the art of painting, and indeed it must embrace masterpieces from every branch of the arts. Much of the most striking work was executed in the area of the Rhine and in the southern duchies, especially Swabia, Franconia and Bavaria—areas studded with rich and flourishing towns. None of these provincial centres, it is true, could rival the sheer concentration of the art of Florence. But in the same way that Borgo S. Sepolcro produced Piero della Francesca or Urbino Raphael and Bramante, so the German cities spasmodically produced a succession of gifted masters. Indeed, a town such as Ulm might easily have rivalled many Italian towns in the quality and diversity of the work produced within its walls.

The history of northern sculpture during the first half of the 15th century is very fragmentary. Although it might be expected to describe a course similar to painting, the subsequent destruction in the Netherlands has been so great that any thesis concerning the development and spread of a French or Burgundian court style cannot be proved because hardly any sculpture survives in the three former centres of Brussels, Bruges or Antwerp. The little that can be deduced of the contemporary taste at Prague

70. **Hans Multscher.** *Madonna and Child.* 1456–8. Frauenkirche, Vipiteno (Sterzing). The central figure from a large altarpiece. The soft flowing drapery patterns of the earlier part of the century have given way to something more angular, the so-called 'crumpled' style. This reached its most fantastic in the work of a man like Veit Stoss (see figure 73).

and Dijon *c.* 1400 shows that at about this time drapery was made both heavier and more exuberant in its patterns. Works in this style can be traced in Germany during the first half of the century at a town such as Nürnberg, although often it lacks the realistic detail and strong emotional expression of Sluter's sculpture. Exceptions existed like Hans Multscher, who has already been mentioned as a painter. His main activity took place in Swabia at Ulm; but in the Tyrol at Vipiteno (formerly Sterzing) there exist the pieces of a large carved altar executed by him in 1456–8. The central figure of the Madonna has an elongated face and serious expression which, though reminiscent of Sluter, may be derived from Flemish painting. Another important point to be noticed is the suggestion of a new drapery convention in the folds around the Virgin's hands and feet. There the decorative pattern becomes more angular and the appearance more crumpled. It is the 'crumpled style' of drapery, again already seen fully developed in Flemish painting, which gives German late medieval sculpture much of its individual character, and this leads directly on to the work of Nikolaus Gerhaert.

Gerhaert worked in Alsace for much of the period between 1463 and 1467 when, at the command of the Emperor Frederick III he moved to Vienna, dying at Wiener Neustadt in 1473. He is thought to have come from Leyden in Holland and, although nothing is known about his training, it is possible that he had travelled in both France and the Netherlands. His range covered sculpture of almost every type; and he had a command of naturalistic detail worthy of Jan van Eyck. Although much of his work is now in a fragmentary state, one feature emerges clearly; his style heralds the appearance in sculpture of a fully developed 'crumpled style' of drapery.

It was probably Gerhaert's work that fixed many of the characteristics of late 15th-century German sculpture. Already before Gerhaert's death, Michael Pacher had begun his masterpiece, the altarpiece at St Wolfgang (1471–81), an ensemble of overwhelming richness. It is worth observing, however, that the central carving of the *Coronation of the Virgin*, in spite of this richness of detail, is not confused. The strong decorative tendencies of the style are set off against an effective use of depth which breaks up the surface into a series of visually comprehensible units. Depth is also employed to give dramatic effects of light and shade; for instance, the two saints flanking the altarpiece emerge from the depths of the recesses in which they stand.

Three men may be mentioned to give an idea of the range and quality of the work produced by the generation of German sculptors succeeding Gerhaert and Pacher. Erasmus Grasser, who worked mainly in and around Munich (Bavaria), in 1480 produced a set of small figures for the decoration of the Rathaus there. Known as 'morris dancers', these figures are all set in elaborate and contrasted poses, and each has an individual physiognomy and expression. Veit Stoss, a contemporary Nürnberg sculptor, was probably a more impressive artist. His figures are

71. **Nikolaus Gerhaert.** *Portrait figure.* c. 1465. Sandstone.
h. 28⅛ in. (41 cm.). Private collection. Very little is known about
Gerhaert although he seems to have been a brilliant sculptor.
This half-length portrait of a man who is either blind or asleep is
an example of the vivid realism of his style.

72. **Erasmus Grasser.** *Morris Dancer.* c. 1480. Wood. Rathaus,
Munich. This sculpted figure is one of a set which forms part of
the lateral decoration of the main council chamber. Each figure
presents a contrasted pose and the set represents an interesting
continuation of the sort of strong characterisation found in the
earlier sculpture of Gerhaert.

remarkable for their vivid expressive faces and the extreme
convolutions of the drapery, which appears at times to be
taking on a life of its own. Of all late Gothic manifestations
73 of the 'crumpled style', the drapery of Veit Stoss is perhaps
the most extreme and individual. The only contemporary
of Stoss to appear now as a serious rival was a sculptor of
Würzburg, Tilmann Riemenschneider. By comparison his
sculpture is restrained in its emotive expression, and his
drapery, while being elaborate, is not violently exaggerated. His faces, although expressive, are not violently over-
emphasised. In any sculpted group restraint makes it easier
for the spectator to understand what is going on. A Riemenschneider altarpiece, indeed, often has the appearance of a
well managed stage set and a considerable amount of
attention was devoted to the problem of making the drama
comprehensible. As a piquant dramatic device, his surviving altarpieces are pierced in the rear wall with tiny
windows to admit light from behind as well as from the
front.

The strength and excellence of northern artistic traditions can now be grasped. Architecture in the late Gothic
tradition of the North was at least as inventive and exciting
as anything found in Italy, whether its culmination is taken
to be the English Perpendicular style or the achievement of
the masons in Germany. The architecture of Brunelleschi
might well have seemed pedestrian to a traveller from

Nürnberg, and the spire of Strasbourg cathedral more   67
spectacular than the dome of Florence cathedral. Would
the interior of the chapel of King's College, Cambridge,   68
have seemed less splendid than the interior of the papal
chapel of Sixtus IV, the Sistine chapel? Differences of   61
approach and taste were, indeed, as fundamental as the
visual differences between Veit Stoss and the contemporary
work of Andrea Sansovino.

SOME EARLY APPROACHES TO ITALIAN RENAISSANCE ART

The assimilation of Italian Renaissance ideas in the North
did not automatically mean complete submission to an
alien style. At the French court the painter Jean Fouquet   69
produced work which bears numerous traces of Italian
influence. During a working life which extended from
c. 1440 to 1481 he visited Rome and probably saw the work
of Piero della Francesca and Fra Angelico. However, the
two most obvious general Italianate features of his paintings
are the spasmodic use of a form of linear perspective and
the frequent appearance of Florentine Quattrocento
architectural features. The striking volume and simplifica-
tions of his painting of heads and limbs is also reminiscent
of Italy. A similar approach is to be found in work attached
to the anonymous master of the altarpiece in the cathedral
of Moulins (the Maître de Moulins); and indeed, in view of

73. **Veit Stoss.** *St Andrew.* c. 1505. Limewood. h. 78¾ in. (200 cm.). St Sebaldus, Nürnberg. The work of Stoss stands out, in a period already full of brilliant and exciting sculpture. The drapery of his figures is perhaps excessively complicated, their faces excessively troubled, but they represent the ultimate development of many features inherent in Gerhaert's work.

the whole course of Italian influence in the North during the previous century, this development might be expected. Northern artists had frequently shown interest in the structure and compositional ideas of Italian painting, while the incorporation of Italian decorative details is also found before this date.

A sculptural work which shows a similar type of influence is the shrine of St Sebaldus at Nürnberg, executed by the Vischer family, mainly between 1508 and 1519. This contains a large amount of small decorative sculpture, some of it clearly deriving from Italian models. Considering the presence of Veit Stoss in Nürnberg at this time, the figure style of the Vischer family is surprising in its simplicity, for in its general appearance it is closer to the decorative sculpture of the earlier 15th century before the 'crumpled style' became pre-eminent. Whether the evident clarification of structure owes anything to Italy is not clear (Hermann Vischer visited Italy in 1515); but the total effect of the shrine is still recognisably northern.

Even the most blatantly characteristic subjects of Italian Renaissance painting could be translated into a northern idiom. The court painter Lukas Cranach who, apart from a brief stay at Vienna, worked most of his life at the Saxon court at Wittenberg, derived a number of ideas from Italian paintings which he must have seen. One of these was a subject familiar from Venetian art, the reclining naked female—a subject apparently popular with the Elector of Saxony. Few people, however, would dismiss Cranach as a feeble plagiarist. The basic idea was translated into his own terms and, in a very personal way, these recumbent nudes have a charm and appeal of their own although entirely unclassical in proportions and recognisably Germanic in their facial types.

THE APPEAL OF THE NEW STYLE FROM ITALY

Towards the end of the 15th century a crucial change gradually took place in the attitude of northerners to Italian art. Assimilation was no longer enough; exact mimesis and reproduction came increasingly to be expected. Italian art became the only fashionable art and compromise with the local tradition was no longer acceptable. The turning point seems to have been reached when it was considered necessary to import Italian artists into the North—a process which was already beginning during the 1490s, when the Florentine Andrea Sansovino visited Portugal at the request of its king. Early in the next century the royal tomb of Henry VII of England was executed by an Italian (Pietro Torrigiano), an event without parallel since the time of Henry III in the 13th century. But of all European courts, the French royal family were probably the most closely acquainted with Italian art since, in the course of the political upheavals of the late 15th and early 16th century, both Charles VIII and Louis XII invaded Italy. It is surely significant to find the funeral monument of Louis XII executed by two Italian brothers, Antonio and Giovanni Giusti (1515–31); whereas at about

74. **The Vischer Family.** *Shrine of St Sebaldus.* 1508–19.
Bronze. St Sebaldus, Nürnberg. This work, an interesting
contrast to the contemporary work of Stoss (also in Nürnberg),
was executed by Peter Vischer the Elder and his two sons Peter
and Hermann. In general outlines the monument is traditional
but the figures are remarkable for their simplicity (contrast Stoss)
and many of the ideas for detail were imported from Italy.

the same date, the Emperor Maximilian was still happy to
entrust the family mausoleum at Innsbruck to various *76*
German artists (1508–33).

The growth of an Italian Renaissance style in the North
must naturally have been assisted by the fact that princely
patrons were impressed by it. But Italian art also had what
may be crudely called a 'selling-point' possessed by no
other European art—it was associated with a literary
tradition which provided not only rules enabling the lay-
man to judge beauty, but also a nascent vocabulary of art
criticism. Italy was already a land of art treatises and a
land in which educated people were prepared to take an
informed interest in the arts. The means existed towards the
end of distinguishing 'right' from 'wrong' in art, as if the
Italians had eaten fruit from a new Tree of Knowledge. As
the 16th century progressed this came increasingly to mean
that any form or work of art based on antique models was
'right', while the rest (which included most northern art
in any form of Gothic idiom) was wrong, although it must
be admitted that a judicious writer such as Vasari admired
the detailed technique of many northern artists.

An interesting story emphasising the apparent 'rightness'
of art derived from the antique was related by Benvenuto
Cellini in his autobiography. While he was serving the
French king the artist Primaticcio persuaded Francis I
to send him to Rome to obtain plaster casts of certain
major pieces of antique sculpture. 'He told the king that,
when his Majesty had once set eyes upon those marvellous
works, he would then, and not till then, be able to criticise
the arts of design, since everything which he had seen by us
moderns was far removed from the perfection of the
ancients.' This approach must have had a very marked
effect on patrons, collectors and connoisseurs. Persistent
propaganda of this nature would ultimately make those
who patronised art in the style of Veit Stoss feel decidedly
uncultivated. The seeds of the Grand Tour had been sown.

The will to imitate the Italian High Renaissance styles
quickly spread to artists themselves, particularly in the
Netherlands—with results which were far from happy. Jan
Gossaert, called Mabuse, a painter who was a little *74*
younger than Cranach, nevertheless provides an interesting
case for comparison. He too was influenced by Italian
models, but having visited Italy in 1508 he experienced his
models at first hand. He certainly possessed the desire to
emulate the classical ideal; but the almost painful Flemish
realism, the painstaking technique and uncertain articula-
tion deprive his figures of charm (unlike the Cranach
nymph). The spectator is left with the impression of heavy
graceless ridicule. Gossaert was the first of a succession of
Netherlandish painters collectively nicknamed 'the Romanists' through their enthusiasm for Roman art, ancient
and modern. This enthusiasm was certainly fostered by the
presence of Raphael's cartoons in Brussels *c.* 1516–19
where the Sistine chapel tapestries were being woven; it

(Continued on page 129)

62. **Albrecht Dürer.** *Self-portrait.* 1498.
Painting on panel. 20½ × 16⅛ in.
(52 × 41 cm.). Prado, Madrid. From

c. 1490 enthusiasm for the learning and
culture of Italy gathered momentum
north of the Alps. One of the earliest
northern artists to devote intense study to
Italian art was Albrecht Dürer. This
self-portrait, painted shortly after his first

visit to Venice, may therefore be regarded
as symbolising the beginning of the
process by which northern art came to be
completely penetrated by ideas and
standards from the south.

63. **Hugo van der Goes.** *The Portinari altarpiece* (right wing). *c.* 1475. 99⅝ × 119⅝ in. (253 × 141 cm.). Uffizi, Florence. It is interesting that, in spite of all differences of taste and style, Flemish painting was prized by Italian business-men and collectors such as the Portinari family. Hugo van der Goes was one of the greatest late 15th-century Flemish artists still recognisably painting in the tradition of van Eyck and Roger van der Weyden.

64. **Bartholomäus Spranger.** *Hercules and Omphale.* 1575–80. Painting on panel. 9½ × 7½ in. (24 × 19 cm.). Kunsthisto-risches Museum, Vienna. Schooled in Antwerp among the Romanists, Spranger moved to Rome and thence to Vienna and Prague. In the course of his life he developed his own personal brand of Italianate painting which, whatever its merits, is far removed from the world of Hugo van der Goes. Such was the magnitude of the influence of Italian art on the North.

NORTHERN ARTISTIC TRADITIONS
IN THE 15TH CENTURY

65. **Michael Pacher.** *The Fathers of the
Church.* Part of an altarpiece from
Neustift (Tyrol). 1482–3. Paint on panel.
Each part *c.* 81 × 36 in. (206 × 91 cm.).
Alte Pinakothek, Munich. At some stage
in his career Michael Pacher experienced
the work of Mantegna and his followers.
Only this explains the emphasis on spatial
definition and the wiry clarity of his style.
In spite of this there is as yet no sign of any
wish to introduce antique motifs.

66. **Michael Pacher.** *The Coronation of
the Virgin.* 1471–81. Centre panel of the
altarpiece of St Wolfgang. Painting on
wood. 153½ × 124½ in. (390 × 316 cm.).
A superb example of a common type of
German altarpiece. Pacher was both
sculptor and painter which may explain
the three-dimensional emphasis of his
painted work. Notable here is the elaboration of the tracery in the canopy, a typical
feature of late 15th-century sculpture and
architecture.

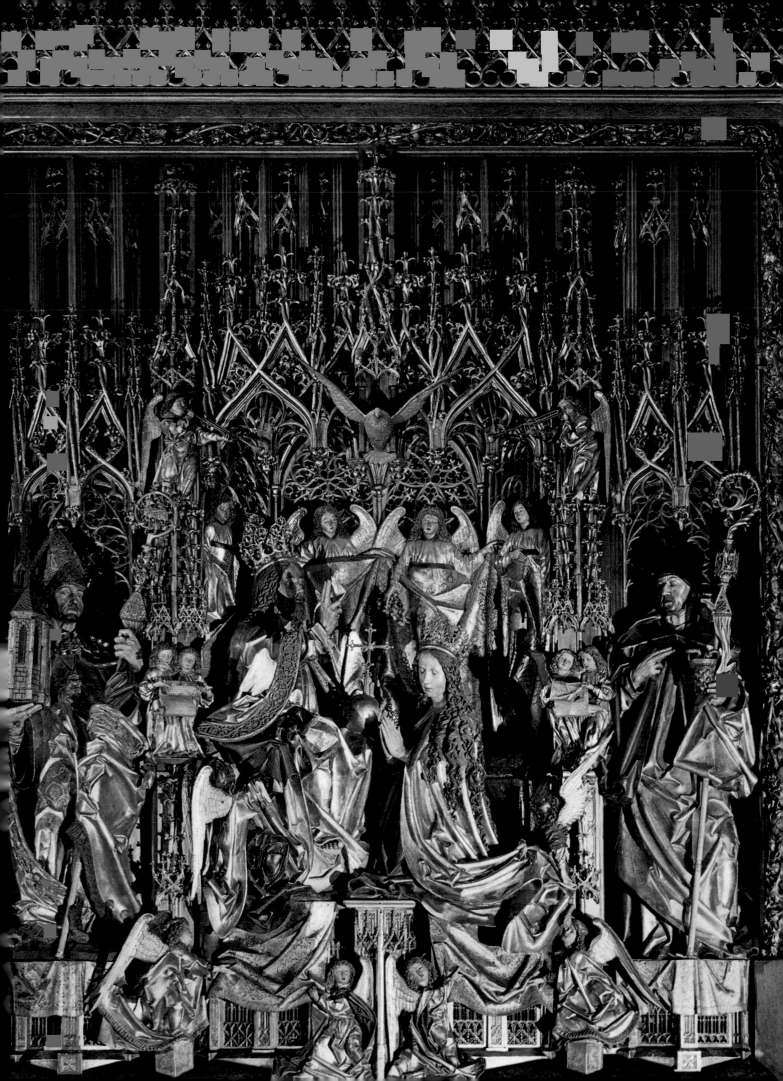

NORTHERN CHURCH INTERIORS

67. *St Lorenz*, Nürnberg. This church, designed and built *c.* 1493, is a 'Hall-church'—a common late Gothic type in which the aisles rise to the same height as the nave. Nürnberg possesses two great churches of this type. St Lorenz is furnished inside with an elaborate Sacrament Tabernacle (1493–6) by Adam Krafft, visible here. Its canopy work may be compared to that of the St Wolfgang altarpiece (plate 66). St Lorenz also possesses various works of Veit Stoss.

68. *The Chapel of King's College*, Cambridge. Planned in the 15th century, this chapel was built mainly between 1508 and 1515. Its construction therefore ran parallel to the earliest phase of the rebuilding of St Peters, Rome. It is one of the most imposing monuments of English Perpendicular architecture and the sumptuous character of the interior underlines the fact that, although built for a collegiate community, it is in fact a royal foundation. The choir screen, added 1533–5, is one of the earliest studies in Italianate detail to survive in England.

69. **Jean Fouquet.** *The Visitation.* A page from the *Hours of Etienne Chevalier.* *c.* 1452–60. Painting on vellum. 6½ × 4¾ in. (16·5 × 12 cm.). Musée Condé, Chantilly. The figure and drapery style belong to the northern tradition but the scenery is Italian—probably Florentine. Notable is the light classical architecture and the wall with cyprus trees beyond—both of which find many parallels in Florentine work of the time. Fouquet has also taken the trouble to imitate, accurately, Albertian perspective.

70. **Lukas Cranach.** *Nymph. c.* 1530. Painting on panel. 28¾ × 43 in. (73 × 109 cm.). Thyssen-Bornemisza Collection, Switzerland. Cranach is famed as a portraitist but he also produced for the court of Saxony a number of erotic pictures based on Venetian prototypes of Giorgione, Titian and Palma Vecchio. The extent to which the painter depended on his Italian examples is debatable. A comparison with Titian (plate 92) would suggest that the idea from the south has been translated into triumphantly German terms.

71. Attributed to **Geertgen tot Sint Jans.**
The Nativity. c. 1490. Painting on panel.
$13\frac{1}{2} \times 9\frac{3}{4}$ in. (34 × 25 cm.). National
Gallery, London. The origins of this
remarkable study in the use of light and
shade are obscure. It remains unique in
northern Europe during the 15th century
and the nearest parallel is Piero della
Francesca's *Dream of Constantine* at
Arezzo (*c.* 1450s). Whatever the nature of
the links between these two works,
Geertgen's minute masterpiece must
occupy a significant place in the history
of painting.

72. **Francesco Primaticcio.** *The Rape of Helen.* Probably 1540s. Painting on canvas. 61¼ × 74¼ in. (155·5 × 188·5 cm.). Bowes Museum, Barnard Castle. A good example of the type of painting practised by artists imported into France by Francis I. The style is ultimately Roman (it makes an interesting comparison with Salviati and Jacopino del Conte—see figures 60, 59) but learnt at second-hand through Giulio Romano and especially Parmigianino (see plate 56). It had great influence on local sculptors.

73. **Benvenuto Cellini.** *The Royal Salt.* Gold, enamel and precious stones. h. 10¼ in. (26 cm.). Kunsthistorisches Museum, Vienna. This famous saltcellar, completed in 1543 and destined for Francis I of France, was based on a model prepared in 1539 for Cardinal d'Este of Ferrara. Like the great fountains of the age, it is elaborate in form and iconography and represents the ocean (Neptune) and earth. The great elegance of the figures compares well with the style of Primaticcio.

124

74 (previous page). **Jan Gossaert (Mabuse).** *Neptune and Amphitrite. c.* 1516. Painting on panel. 74 × 48¾ in. (188 × 124 cm.). State Museums, Berlin-Dahlem. Early Flemish attempts to imitate Italian art at all closely often appear ludicrous to modern eyes. In spite of this, it is true that artists from Flanders remained among the most avid followers of the cult of Italy and the antique. To this passion we owe many works of minor significance such as the beautiful topographical sketches of the city of Rome by Heemskerck. From this area emerged, later in the century, important artists such as Spranger (plate 64) and Adriaen de Vries (plate 75).

75. **Adriaen de Vries.** *The Hercules Fountain*, Augsburg. 1602. Among the early works of de Vries are two large fountains executed for Augsburg. One of these, the Hercules fountain, is reminiscent

of another Hercules fountain, that of Giovanni Bologna at Bologna. Since de Vries learnt under Giovanni Bologna in Florence his sculptural style is understandably similar. Artists such as de Vries and monuments such as this fountain played an important part in propagating a truly Italianate style.

76. **Wenzel Jamnitzer.** *Spring*. Bronze. h. *c.* 28 in. (71 cm.). Kunsthistorisches Museum, Vienna. One of four allegorical figures forming part of a fountain executed for the imperial court. The work of Jamnitzer from *c.* 1545, like the later works of Spranger, marks the full acceptance of the Habsburg family of an Italianate style for their court commissions. The exact sources of Jamnitzer are obscure but his figures clearly belong to the same stylistic group as those of Parmigianino, Primaticcio and Cellini (see plates 56, 72 and 73).

77. **Pierre Lescot.** *Façade of the Louvre*,
Paris. *c.* 1546. Part of the new building of
the Louvre, begun *c.* 1546, this façade is
remarkable for its careful dignity and
restraint. Its virtues are not perhaps fully
apparent until comparisons are made
with other contemporary buildings such
as Somerset House, London (figure 81)
or the castle at Heidelberg (see below).
No building, however, could match the
unexpected grandeur and massive
classicism of the palace of Charles V at
Granada (see figure 83).

78. *The Ottheinrichsbau*, Heidelberg.
1556–9. Like many early essays in a new
style, there are many excesses and mis-
understandings here, and a *horror vacui*
reminiscent of certain phases of medieval
art. Comparison with the palace of
Charles V (figure 83) or the Escorial will
emphasise the riotous but rather thin
nature of the applied classical detail.

NORTHERN LANDSCAPE PAINTING

79. **Albrecht Altdorfer.** *Danube Landscape. c.* 1520. Painting on panel. 12 × 8¾ in. (30·5 × 22 cm.). Alte Pinakothek, Munich. Northern landscape painting often seems to be epitomised in the work of Breughel. He had, however, many predecessors including Geertgen tot Sint Jans, Patenir and Dürer all of whom,

in different ways, devoted particular attention to painting of the countryside. Albrecht Altdorfer, in a completely different part of Germany, was also a highly individual landscape artist, producing evocative studies of pine-clad hills and mountain lakes. Normally at this date a token figure subject was still attached to a painting, but here the landscape has taken complete control.

80. **Pieter Breughel the Elder.** *Landscape with Gallows*. Signed and dated 1568. Painting on panel. 18 × 20 in. (46 × 51 cm.). Hessisches Landesmuseum, Darmstadt. The subject-matter of Breughel's paintings is frequently enigmatic. Here the beauty of the landscape and the harmless games of the children seem deliberately contrasted with the gaunt shape of the empty gallows. In common with much of Breughel's work, the beauty of the scene probably holds also a simple moral message.

was also stimulated by frequent journeys to Italy. Thus Jan van Scorel of Utrecht travelled there in 1520–4, Scorel's pupil Maerten van Heemskerck in 1532 and Bernard van Orley of Brussels at some unknown date. At this point, therefore, a further number of 'un-Flemish' features appear in the painting of northern artists—heavy nude studies, striking foreshortening, conscientiously contrasted figure poses, and heavy, Bramantesque architectural detail.

DÜRER AND ITALY

The oppressive influence of Italy is also to be found in the career of a far greater artist than any of the 'Romanists'. That artist was Albrecht Dürer, a native of Nürnberg whose works therefore should be set alongside those of Veit Stoss and the Vischer family. Dürer was trained as a painter and engraver in the current post-Rogerian style *c.* 1486–9. He was indeed an admirer of the great engraver Martin Schongauer of Colmar who had in his turn been much influenced by the style of Roger van der Weyden. This early training left a permanent impression on Dürer's work although he assimilated many ideas from Italy. Dürer is indeed a good example of a great artist whose work remained triumphantly northern in character, in spite of the fact that he investigated the basis of Italian art more profoundly than any of his German contemporaries. Perhaps this was precisely because he was not willing to be merely a superficial imitator. Dürer visited Italy twice (1494–5 and 1505–7) and between these visits he became fascinated by the theories of art emanating from Italy. Perhaps during the first Italian journey he met the Venetian artist Jacopo de' Barbari who showed him two drawings of a man and a woman 'constructed by means of measurement', but who refused to divulge what these measurements were. Dürer seems to have thought for a short while that the Italians had discovered artistic secrets which would provide some sort of key to beauty. There followed an idealistic phase in Dürer's career which culminated in the *Adam and Eve* engraving of 1504. In this, apart from Eve's face, the general impression is extremely Italianate. Eventually Dürer's attitude to the theory of human proportion developed far beyond this simple search for a single ideal; but the striking feature is that he accepted the Italian idea that 'good art' has rules, and that these rules could be the subject of academic analysis to be reduced to textbook formulas.

77

81 (opposite). **Hans Holbein.** *Henry VIII.* 1542. Oil and tempera on wood. 86½ × 26¼ in. (219 × 66 cm.). George Howard Collection, Castle Howard, Yorkshire. One of Holbein's later and most magnificent court portraits. This type of portrait is a status picture, underlining the position of the sitter by the splendour of his clothing. It has much in common with Bronzino's court portraits of the Medici and with the work of imperial artists such as Jakob Seisenegger. Holbein's brilliant technique was well suited to this style of work but his most sensitive portraits were of sitters like the More family, with more sympathetic characters.

75. **Antonio** and **Giovanni Giusti.** *Tomb of Louis XII.* 1515–31. Marble. St Denis, Paris. Although the attribution of the total design of this monument is not entirely settled, the presence of Italian sculptors at the French court was symptomatic of a change of attitude in France towards the artistic taste of Italy. From now on Francis I tried systematically to propagate an authentic classical style in France and imported Italian artists for this purpose.

76. *Tomb of Maximilian I.* 1508–33. Bronze. Hofkirche, Innsbruck. Many different German sculptors took part in this project in which the dead man was shown surrounded by illustrious ancestors. The 'family genealogy' is an old motif in north European art, and in general this monument followed northern traditions (contrast figure 75).

77. **Albrecht Dürer.** *Adam and Eve.* 1504. Engraving.
9¾ × 7½ in. (24 × 19 cm.). This probably represents Dürer at his
most Italianate, although the detail of the background foliage
and Eve's face to some extent counteract this impression. The
derivation of Adam's figure is, however, unmistakable. Dürer
was the first northern artist to try to master the theory of
Italian art.

78. **Mathias Grünewald.** *Crucifixion. c.* 1524. Pinewood.
77 × 60 in. (195·5 × 152·5 cm.). Badische Kunsthalle,
Karlsruhe. Grünewald's own brand of realism was unsparing in
its intensity, and emerges particularly in his representations
of Christ's Passion.

As a result he compiled *Four Books on Human Proportion*
(published shortly after his death); and other works were
projected but never written, such as a treatise on architecture. The tone of his writing is by turns humble and
pedagogic, and underlying it all is the assumption that
there is a 'right' and a 'wrong' in art which can be distinguished when the intellect comes to the aid of technical
expertise.

This aspect of Dürer's Italianism is frequently emphasised both for its intrinsic interest and on account of its unexpected appearance in a non-Italian artist at this date.
Dürer's reputation in his own time, however, rested on his
skill as an artist, particularly as an engraver. It was widely
recognised on both sides of the Alps that he had raised the
art of engraving to a new level. But he was seen as one
German artist among others; and shortly after his death
his friend, the humanist Melanchthon, thought it not inappropriate to compare him directly to Cranach and
Grünewald (1531). This may now seem surprising. Grünewald, a shadowy personality, painted in an extraordinary
and vivid style. For instance, his unforgettable representations of the *Crucifixion* are horrific and unsparing in their
savage detail, and it may seem difficult to imagine how
the smallest acquaintance with his painting could fail to
separate his style from that of Dürer. However it did not
occur to Melanchthon to see them as opposites; he took the

grandeur of Dürer's style and opposed to it the grace of
Cranach's, adding that Grünewald held a middle course
between the two. This is interesting since it can only mean
that in 1531 the idea of the unity of the German Gothic
tradition was still a commonplace. In spite of Dürer's own
personal interest in Italian ideas and Cranach's interpretation of Italian themes, Italianism and classicism were
still of small importance in any critical assessment of style.
Dürer and Cranach were first and foremost the heirs of a
German tradition which they held in common with
Grünewald.

FONTAINEBLEAU—THE DEVELOPMENT OF FRENCH RENAISSANCE ART

One by one the north European courts fell under the spell
of antique art. It seems likely that in this process the increasing prestige enjoyed by classical scholarship and
letters played a considerable part, but the influence of
letters on the visual arts is often hard to trace. The most
prominent centre in the general tendency to emulate
Italian achievements in the arts was certainly France where
the kings consistently extended their patronage to Italian
artists throughout the first half of the century. The chief of
these royal patrons was Francis I who began by patronising
the unequal talents of the Giusti brothers and Leonardo
da Vinci (1517). The series of artists should have included

78

79

79. *Francis I. c.* 1530. Oil on canvas. 39¾ × 29 in. (96 × 74 cm.). Louvre, Paris. Painted here by an unidentified artist, in the past thought to be Jean Clouet, Francis I was the first French king to patronise, determinedly and consistently, artists from Italy. The rebuilding of Fontainebleau was begun by him, and under his patronage the first phase of 'Fontainebleau Mannerism' developed.

80. **Primaticcio.** *Detail from the Chambre de la Duchesse d'Etampes,* Fontainebleau. *c.* 1541–5. Paint and stucco. This illustrates well some of the features of 'Fontainebleau Mannerism'. The figures are extremely attenuated and elegant, and the decoration is exuberant. Noteworthy are the huge plaster scrolls, known as 'strap-work', which here make their first major appearance in west European art.

Fra Bartolommeo who, however, declined an invitation, and Andrea del Sarto who accepted, but stayed less than a year (1518–19); and the architect and sculptor Jacopo Sansovino was also lost to the French court, because in the course of the journey he was persuaded to stay permanently in Venice (1529). Eventually the first important Italian artists who radically changed the appearance of French court art were Rosso Fiorentino, who arrived in 1530, and the Bolognese Primaticcio, who arrived from Mantua in 1532.

By this date Francis I was already enlarging and improving his hunting lodge at Fontainebleau and, as a result of the concentrated activity there during the next decades, the works of art executed for him are usually referred to collectively as being of the 'Fontainebleau school', the style being called 'Fontainebleau Mannerism'. The work required from Rosso and Primaticcio was mainly of a decorative character and, drawing from a joint experience of Mantua and Rome, they produced schemes of decoration in a fascinating and wholly individual style. Many of these **72** still survive; their character is fantastic, elegant and extravagant. One feature which was apparently new and contributed to the richness of each room is the consistent com-**80** bination of painting and moulded stucco work, which was treated for the first time in immense curling scrolls (generally called 'strapwork').

A later arrival at the French court was that flamboyant personality Benvenuto Cellini who paid a brief visit in **73** 1537, and then stayed permanently from 1540 to 1545. His style has much in common with that of Primaticcio who became his great rival at Fontainebleau. Cellini's two main surviving works from this period are the elaborate gold saltcellar (already begun in Rome in 1539) and the bronze lunette relief more generally known as the 'Nymph of Fontainebleau' (1543–4). In both, the figure style is attenuated as in the work of Primaticcio; and the saltcellar has an elaborate allegorical iconography which Cellini himself explains in his writings.

The presence of these Italian artists and others such as the architect Serlio (who arrived *c.* 1540–1) assisted the precocious development of a native classicising style. This can be appreciated by comparing the exterior of the Louvre palace as it was rebuilt *c.* 1546 with contemporary building at other northern courts. The Louvre façade was designed by a French scholar-architect Pierre Lescot and, with its **77** rather flat monotonous surface, is not perhaps very inspiring. Comparisons with Alberti's Rucellai palace spring **26** to mind. However two further palaces exist, which bring out the inherent restraint and discipline of Lescot's design and emphasise his great understanding of the Italian models which he used. One is the palace built in London at **81** about the same date by the Lord Protector of England,

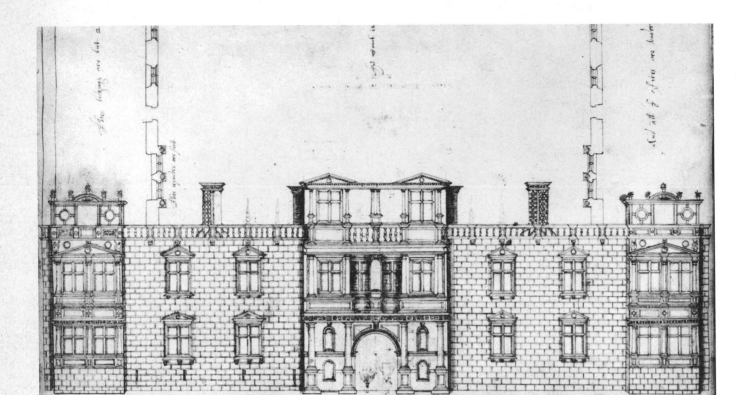

81. **John Thorpe.** *The Strand façade of Somerset House, London.*
Early 17th century. Drawing. 10¾ × 16¾ in. (27 × 43 cm.).
The Soane Museum, London. The palace was built 1547–52
and no longer exists. It presents the first attempt at a wholly
Italianate piece of building in England, although most of its
decorative ideas stemmed in the first place from France.

Somerset, which by comparison with the Louvre seems
weak and incoherent. The other is at Heidelberg where,
78 on the other hand, that part of the castle built (*c.* 1556–9)
by Prince Otto Heinrich, Count Palatine of the Rhine, is
overpoweringly ornate.

The Frenchman Philibert de l'Orme was a far greater
architect than the careful designer of the Louvre. He came
from a family of masons, and early in his life visited Italy,
including Rome (*c.* 1533), where he completed a first-hand
survey of classical remains. On his return he received em-
ployment from the French king on a wide range of projects;
but he also compiled a treatise on architecture which was
first published in 1567. As with the case of Dürer, the idea
of a treatise was Italian; but it is soon apparent (again as
with Dürer) that the writer was not merely a slavish imitator of Italy. Both de l'Orme's writing and his building make
it plain that French artists were now developing an individual version of the classical style.

The Italianate background which produced these architects also produced two outstanding sculptors. The first,
65 Jean Goujon, collaborated with Lescot at the Louvre. His
range of expression was limited but during the middle
years of the century he developed a restrained and personal
brand of classicism, which is certainly not the work of a

hesitant northerner playing with something new and half
understood. The sculpture of Germain Pilon has greater
variety. By comparison with Goujon his figures are heavier **82**
and his drapery more exuberant, but his work is nevertheless always elegant. It is clear that he had completely
mastered the grammar of Renaissance sculpture and that,
as with architecture, the French were on the way to
developing an individual sculptural style in the classical
idiom.

During the course of the 16th century it becomes increasingly difficult to follow and explain the spread of
classical and Italianate ideas in Western art. The fantastic
decorative ideas developed at Fontainebleau were themselves widely copied, for Fontainebleau was more easily
accessible to many northern artists than Italy; and moreover the ideas evolved by Rosso and Primaticcio received
wide publicity through the medium of engravings. This
phenomenon was not confined to France because ever since
the last years of the 15th century the publication of ornament, figures and scenes in the form of engravings had
become increasingly popular both north and south of the
Alps. The idea of 'publication' followed in the wake of the
invention of printing and, as the 16th century proceeded, it
became increasingly common.

82. **Germain Pilon.** *The Risen Christ.* Begun *c.* 1583. St Paul-St Louis, Paris. Part of a sculptural complex intended for the Valois chapel, St Denis (chapel never completed). Although strongly influenced both by the Italians of Fontainebleau and by Michelangelo, he mastered the style to the extent of being able to use it for his own strongly personal and at times emotional purposes.

RENAISSANCE ART AND THE EMPIRE

The patronage of the imperial court during the 16th century ran a somewhat erratic course. The emperors never employed Italian artists with the single-mindedness of the French kings although, admittedly, they used Italian artists while in Italy itself, and Charles V had a great respect for the portraiture of Titian. But there seems to have been little desire for a strongly classicising form of art; and consequently Renaissance ideas arrived by circuitous routes. For instance, Wenzel Jamnitzer, the chief gold- **76** smith to the imperial court (from *c.* 1545), handled a figure style akin to those of Cellini and Primaticcio with elegance and assurance. A craftsman of Nürnberg, he apparently never travelled widely and he must have learnt his style at second hand from drawings and engravings.

The establishment of a living classical artistic tradition in Germany was the work not of visiting Italians nor of enthusiastic Germans, but of itinerant Netherlandish artists. Two great artists were working for the imperial court at the end of the 16th century. One of these, Bartholo- mäus Spranger, came originally from Antwerp. By way of **64** Paris and Lyon he travelled to Italy (1565–6) where he worked successively in Parma and Rome. Eventually, through the mediation of his fellow-Fleming, Giovanni Bologna, he went to Vienna (1575) to serve the Emperor Maximilian II and finally (1576) Rudolf II. Thus the court painter of Vienna and Prague in the last quarter of the century had experience of Parisian court art as well as the work of Correggio and Parmigianino, and of the entire gamut of Roman art from the Sistine ceiling and the *Stanze* up to his departure. From these sources he evolved a style which is characterised by the softness of its technique. It seems likely that his early experience of the work of Correggio and Parmigianino left a permanent impression.

Another Habsburg court artist was the sculptor Adriaen de Vries who came from The Hague. Like Spranger he moved to Italy early in his life and worked under Giovanni Bologna in Florence. After a period of years spent in Rome and Turin he moved to Augsburg (1596) and thence to the court of Rudolf II at Prague (1601). Already in Italy (1593) he had produced some small bronzes for the emperor which show a complete mastery of the style of Giovanni Bologna; and it was through the influence of work such as his two Augsburg fountains (*Mercury* and *Hercules*) that an in- **75** dependent classical sculpture style developed in Germany.

It is impossible here to follow all the significant developments of Renaissance art throughout Europe, but of the German princes the Electors of Bavaria deserve mention. The Elector Albert V, in direct imitation of Italian princes, built an Antiquarium (or Museum for his collections) in an elaborate Italianate style between 1569 and 1571. Later (1581–6) the Elector William V built the Grottenhof of the Munich Residenz and installed in its centre a fountain by another great Italianising sculptor from the Netherlands, Hubert Gerhard (1590). One of Gerhard's masterpieces, a figure of St Michael (1588), is on the façade of the Michaels-

83. **Pedro Machuca.** *Palace of Charles V, Granada.* Probably built from 1539 onwards. Little is known about the architect but his façade has all the heaviness and monumentality of Bramante's architecture. Machuca may have used ideas publicised by the Italian architect Serlio but the massiveness with which they are used distinguishes this design from other contemporary Italianate palaces outside Italy (contrast figure 81 and plates 77 and 78).

kirche in Munich, and this church is itself one of the more important architectural monuments of German Renaissance art. Again it was designed by a Netherlandish architect working in a classical style, Friedrich Sustris. At this stage two general observations may be made. Firstly, the spectacle of these major works of art of the 'German' Renaissance executed by Netherlandish artists reminds one that, however pedestrian the art of the 'Romanists' may seem, the Netherlands remained one of the main European centres of enthusiasm for Italian art. Secondly, the uncertain beginnings of German Renaissance art and its late development meant that the first great classicising monuments by northern artists in Germany were heavily influenced by late 16th-century Italian art. And so, as in the case of Gerhard, when an Italianate classicising style was at long last wholly accepted in Germany, it was already almost baroque.

RENAISSANCE ART IN SPAIN

By the late 15th century Spanish sculpture and architecture had developed into a rich and fantastically ornamented Gothic style, and although Italianate motifs were increasingly introduced they naturally create a rather bizarre impression. Until the second half of the century art produced in Spain continued to have a strongly provincial flavour and with few exceptions there was no real understanding of the ideas underlying the Italian classical revival. As in Germany, this may in part be explained by the lack of a tradition of continuous court patronage; but even when the Habsburg Spanish wealth was poured into artistic enterprises, there is no clear evidence of a consistent royal taste. Philip II collected the strange works of Bosch; but when El Greco came to Spain in 1577 the strangeness of *his* work failed to interest Philip. Philip had a large number of paintings by Titian; but to decorate the Escorial palace in 1585 he summoned three Roman painters reared in the style of Pierino del Vaga and Salviati. Of these three he developed a preference for an artist called Pellegrino Tibaldi.

The formality surrounding the Habsburg court is legendary and some echo of it might be expected in the art patronised there. This is perhaps visible in the work of Tibaldi and his companions. But if comparison is made with the work of contemporary Spanish sculptors, then it is much more obvious in those works commissioned from the Leoni family in Milan. Among other things, Leone Leoni and his son Pompeo executed two large bronze kneeling groups of the families of Charles V and Philip II for the mausolea in the Escorial.

It was presumably a fundamental dislike of the excited ornamental taste peculiar to Spanish art which led Charles V and Philip II to commission two palaces which succeed in being not only totally different from any other contemporary buildings in Spain but also extremely unusual in the context of European architecture.

The first of these is the palace built by Charles V at Granada. The architect was the Spaniard Pedro Machuca, of whom little is known, although the palace was built probably in the years following 1539. If this date is correct the palace was unique outside Italy; for not even Lescot at the Louvre had grasped so clearly the essential character of the Roman architecture of Bramante and his followers.

84

84. **Alonso Berruguete.** *The Transfiguration.* 1543–8. Toledo cathedral. Berruguete had visited Italy earlier in his career (*c.* 1508–17) and his style was much influenced by Italian forms, ideas and ornament. However, like many native Spanish sculptors, he developed an excited and agitated manner which had the effect of introducing a kind of baroque extravagance into his style.

really is because these gestures and movement combined with Italianate detail are things associated more readily with the 17th century than with the mid 16th.

PORTRAITS AND LANDSCAPES

The 16th century was not, on the whole, an outstanding century for north European painting. There were two creative poles, one represented by Cranach who absorbed Italian ideas into his own individual style and the other by Spranger who had mastered a truly Italianate style of his own; and much of the painting produced in France and the Netherlands fell uncomfortably between these two aspirations and became merely Italianate imitation. It is not surprising, therefore, that on the whole artists excelled in those forms of painting which were relatively unaffected by the revived classicism coming from the south. Two such forms were landscape painting and portraiture. Northern Europe continued to produce distinguished portrait painters in the 16th century, including Massys, Gossaert and Jean Clouet: but none of these excelled Hans Holbein, 79 the Swiss artist from Basle. Holbein was able to record with extraordinary ability the detailed appearance and texture of a sitter's costume in an age when, both in Italy and in the North, great importance was attached to such detail. But added to this he had the uncanny ability—common to all great portrait painters—of being able to respond to some aspect of his sitter's personality and then to fix this with some characteristic glance or expression. Thus Holbein's portraits have constant and subtle variations which 81 endow them with unusual interest and vitality.

Towards the end of the 15th century landscape came to be treated more deliberately as an independent subject for the artist. This is already apparent in the work of Geertgen and David, where the subject-matter of a painting was sometimes reduced to exiguous proportions. In the work of artists such as Joachim Patenir and Albrecht Altdorfer at 85, 79 the beginning of the 16th century, a fantastic, imaginary countryside might now occupy the whole canvas where, in the 15th century, it would probably merely have been glimpsed through a window or behind a group of figures. The recording of landscape too now became more com-

Architectural motifs, which Lescot applied rather like a decorative skin, here assume a weight and plasticity appropriate to their function. The simplicity and directness of this style left no apparent trace on Spanish architecture; and its stylistic successor was again a royal palace, the Escorial. The planning, design and execution were again the work of Spaniards—Juan Bautista de Toledo and Juan de Herrera, and work began in 1562. The style again echoes Roman architecture but the scale of execution, the complexity of the plan and the general austerity of the style make it exceptional in Europe. Not even in Italy can satisfactory parallels be found. Here, therefore, between the solemn formality of court taste and the exceptional liveliness and emotion of traditional preference were the makings of a highly individual classical style of the 17th century.

Native Spanish painting and sculpture tended towards a more intense emotional expression than the tastes of the Habsburg monarchs allowed (it was probably this which Philip II found distasteful in the painting of El Greco). A species of 'proto-baroque' art is already visible by the middle of the century in the work of Alonso Berruguete. He had visited Italy, probably between 1508 and 1517, and on his return he rapidly evolved a personal style without exact parallels in contemporary Europe. The key to the understanding of this style seems to lie in the fact that he shed the trappings of Spanish Gothic art but expressed the same highly pitched emotion in the classicising dress of Italian art. Thus in the *Transfiguration* made for the high 84 altar of Toledo cathedral (1543–8) the group has the superficial appearance of being much later in date than it

mon, as can be seen in the drawings of Dürer. The connections with Italy are not at all clear; for although northern artists certainly influenced the Italians, it is also true that the earliest surviving drawing of an actual landscape is the 1473 *Arno Valley* by Leonardo da Vinci. Many Italian painters were extremely sensitive to the beauties of the natural world and no survey of landscape painting could ignore the success of Venetian artists in making a landscape background convey a mood to support the subject-matter of the painting (see p. 140). But of all northern landscape artists of the 16th century the greatest was probably Pieter Breughel. His early style is close to the tradition of Bosch and an element of satire persists throughout his work. However his mature paintings show an unprecedented interest in the countryside and its inhabitants. Trained in Antwerp, he travelled to Italy in 1552–3 and penetrated as far as Sicily. During the course of this journey he certainly visited Rome, but he is distinguished by the fact that classical Italy apparently made no impression on him at all. His satirical pictures of the countryside and country life, so different from any contemporary work in Italy, are fre-

quently obscure in their precise meaning; but since these vivid evocations of the more earthy aspects of rustic life were appreciated and collected by members of the Spanish ruling hierarchy during Breughel's life-time, it is unlikely that their intention is ever subversive or heretical. Breughel, like Bosch, was probably producing personal meditations on such general subjects as the folly of mankind which he illustrated from his insight into rural life.

CONCLUSION

The history of Renaissance art in northern Europe of the 16th century must remain inconclusive for reasons already suggested. The spread of Italian ideas was uneven and in certain countries, notably England, extremely spasmodic and unpredictable and almost always through a foreign intermediary. For instance the first English architectural treatise of Italianate usage by John Shute (1563) was heavily influenced from Flanders. Nevertheless by 1580 the transforming influence of Italy was almost everywhere apparent and the story was completed in the following century.

85. **Joachim Patenir.** *Landscape with St Jerome.* 1515. Paint on panel. 29 × 35¾ in. (74 × 91 cm.). Prado, Madrid.
Patenir was one of the first painters to concentrate wholly on landscape painting—even to the extent of getting other artists

occasionally to paint the figures of the subject-matter. Here the subject, St Jerome, is insignificant in the total expanse of the setting which includes a small town and some of the strange rock formations peculiar to Patenir's style.

The Venetian Renaissance

The development of Renaissance art in the republic of Venice may be studied with a satisfactory sense of completeness. Apart from Florence, Venice was the only Italian city with a continuous history of first class artistic creation throughout the period under consideration. Elsewhere, as we have seen, individual cities and courts (occasionally) harboured artists of distinction and temporarily became centres for the diffusion of a particular style before lapsing back into provincial status (the court of Urbino in the 15th century is an example). The republic of Venice throughout this period managed to train or to attract a long succession of distinguished artists most of whom seem to have enjoyed life in Venice sufficiently to stay permanently.

The reasons for this are to be sought at two levels. First, Venice possessed an unusual political system combining rigidity with stability. By the late 15th century, the Doge was little more than a figure-head and the real power was held by a Council of Ten. Membership of the Council was elective, but the whole system was controlled by a small aristocratic oligarchy. Power was maintained by a devious but efficient system of informers and all threats to security from within were promptly and usually secretly dealt with.

This ruthless police system had its compensations. Since the touchstone of all things was state security, things which did not threaten the state tended to be permitted. There was, in fact, a permissive attitude in Venice to nonconformity hardly to be experienced elsewhere in Italy. Such an attitude was designed to foster trade relations and was indeed essential in a city where Germans from the North rubbed shoulders with Turks from the East. Venice possessed a free cosmopolitan atmosphere not to be found anywhere else.

The oligarchic government promoted continuity. Trade promoted wealth and diversity and these provided the second advantage for artists. Such a setting provided any artist with a rich visual experience and the possibility of large financial rewards. The state and the great religious confraternities or scuole were assiduous patrons of the arts, and although they replaced the major types of private patronage, private individuals still commissioned and bought large numbers of smaller religious works and altarpieces.

86. **Antonio Lombardo.** *A Miracle of St Antony of Padua.* 1505. Marble. Detail of decoration of the Capella del Santo, S. Antonio, Padua. The Lombardi family of masons and sculptors were among the most perceptive of the classicising artists of the late 15th century. The style of this relief, both in the drapery and in the facial types, is perhaps more convincingly antique than any other piece of sculpture in this book, and it has a dignity and restraint typical of Venetian art at this period.

87. **Tullio Lombardo.** *Tomb of the Doge Andrea Vendramin.*
c. 1490. Marble. Formerly in Sta Maria dei Servi, later
transferred to SS. Giovanni e Paolo, Venice. This enormous
monument is really a triumphal arch adapted to serve another
purpose. The quality of the sculpture varies but the general
style is similar to figure 86. The best sculpture is of a very high
quality (see figure 88).

88. **Tullio Lombardo.** *Adam. c.* 1490. Marble. h. 76 in.
(193 cm.). Metropolitan Museum of Art, New York. Formerly
part of the tomb of the Doge Andrea Vendramin (figure 87).
One might suppose that Tullio Lombardo had had before his
eyes a genuine work of Praxiteles, so skilfully handled is the
surface of this marble body. It is a sad fact that the
corresponding figure of *Eve* has now vanished.

The tradition of Gothic art in Venice was a strong one
and, as in most centres of north Italy, it survived up to the
middle of the 15th century. It is seen in a monument such
as the *Porta della Carta* of the Doges' Palace (1438–42) or in
the paintings of Jacobello del Fiore and Antonio Vivarini
(*c.* 1420–50). As with many other Italian centres, the
transforming impetus came from Padua although the
degrees by which it was accepted were not the same in
painting and sculpture.

THE LOMBARDO FAMILY

In sculpture and architecture the chief agents of change
were a non-Venetian family of masons called the Lombardi. The father, Pietro Lombardo, came originally from
Carona (northern Lombardy). He is known to have been
in Padua in 1464 and he probably settled in Venice during
this decade. Much of his work survives and, while it is clear
that he could not or would not purge Venetian monuments
and buildings of their ornate character, he did radically
revise the architectural detail and general form of the work
he undertook in response to an archaeological enthusiasm
which he must have developed at Padua. In his monument

to the Doge Pietro Mocenigo (died 1476) in SS. Giovanni e
Paolo he adopted a form of niched architecture based on a
triumphal arch; and, since Mocenigo had been a successful
general, he filled the niches with warriors which are very
similar to the Roman soldiers painted by Mantegna. The
most successful elements in the design are probably the
decorative details, and it is clear from these that Pietro
Lombardo had a highly sensitive appreciation of the visual
character of antique sculpture—an appreciation hard to
match before this date except in the Tempio Malatesta at
Rimini.

This appreciation was shared by Pietro's two sons Antonio and Tullio, and between them they were responsible
for a group of works whose very personal classicism sets
them in a class apart from contemporary developments in
the rest of Italy. One of these was the monument to the
Doge Andrea Vendramin (*c.* 1490, SS. Giovanni e Paolo).
Apart from its enormous size, it is designed on a larger
scale than its predecessors. The detail is less fussy, the individual parts are larger in relation to the whole, and the
design is developed in depth so that the central arch
projects well forward from the main body of the monument.

89. *Part of façade of the Scuola di S. Marco*, Venice. 1488–90. This façade represents one of the earliest surviving illusionistic exterior schemes of decoration. It is remarkable for its scale and simplicity, and it seems likely that it must have influenced 16th-century painters. (See detail, plate 84.)

90. **Jacopo Bellini.** *Christ before Pilate. c.* 1455. Pen and ink. 17 × 11½ in. (43 × 29 cm.). Louvre, Paris. From one of Jacopo Bellini's drawing books. These drawings display a fascination for the new art of perspective. They also show a somewhat erratic and wayward taste for antique details. Both of these features probably reflect the influence of Jacopo's son-in-law, Mantegna.

All these changes represent a more mature appreciation of the grandeur of ancient Rome. In addition to all this, however, the sculpture intended for the monument shows at its best a masterly understanding of antique carving. The figure of *Adam* (now separated from its original destination) shows a most unexpected appreciation of the essential softness of Praxitelean sculpture and like Michelangelo's *Bacchus* it seems to be based on the *Bacchus* of Praxiteles (now known only through copies).

A second major work of the Lombardo family was the rebuilding of the Scuola di S. Marco (*c.* 1490). Here the unexpected innovation was in the lower part of the façade, which was treated like an enormous piece of illusionistic relief sculpture. The right-hand entrance is flanked by two scenes from the life of St Mark which take place in spacious receding loggias with heavily coffered ceilings. The figures, dressed in drapery of a classical type, are probably deliberately dwarfed by the massive piers of the colonnade, so that the scenes are played out in an atmosphere of austere grandeur.

A further monument on which the Lombardo family worked was the chapel of St Anthony in the church of S. Antonio at Padua. Here it was intended to portray scenes from the life of St Anthony in narrative reliefs whose style and setting would have been similar to the reliefs on the Scuola di S. Marco. The Lombardo family only completed a few reliefs, however, the rest following piecemeal as the 16th century progressed. But those which they executed show again their unerring instinct for conveying the measure and gravity of an antique work.

MANTEGNA AND VENETIAN ART

The influence of Mantegna as a source of this classicising style is clear. Mantegna's influence on Venetian painting was equally important, although the total effect was less complete. This influence is to be seen in two particular ways. First, his mastery of pictorial structure had a profound effect on both the lay-out of scenes and the paintings of figures and drapery. This is as easily seen in the early work of Giovanni Bellini as in the painting of Bartolommeo Vivarini. It is also to be seen in the drawings of Giovanni's father, Jacopo Bellini, which show a sudden enthusiasm for enormous vistas and fantastic perspective constructions. Mantegna's influence also emerges in a passing enthusiasm for archaeological detail. In Jacopo Bellini's drawings classical details and objects of a classical character appear alongside his compositional studies; and in the very early work of Giovanni Bellini antique monuments and arches occasionally intrude into the background in a manner reminiscent of Mantegna. These links are not surprising because Jacopo Bellini had agreed in 1453 to the marriage of his daughter to Mantegna, who thus became Giovanni Bellini's brother-in-law.

However, the brilliant style of Mantegna's painting did not overwhelm Venetian painters. Although Giovanni Bellini adopted many of the formal devices of Mantegna so that, for instance, his figures for a brief period take on the statuesque appearance of Mantegna's style, his feeling for colour was never dominated by his brother-in-law. Almost any comparison will always show that Bellini had a greater sensitivity for the overall colour harmony of a painting—a feature characteristic of Venetian painting.

ANTONELLO DA MESSINA

There was one outside artist who affected Venetian painters in the way that they used paint and colour—as opposed to the way that they looked at ruins or drew perspective. This was the Sicilian painter Antonello da Messina. Although there are still numerous problems connected with his career, he seems to have been influenced by Flemish painting. His work also contains hints of the influence of Piero della Francesca but without conclusive connections. In 1475–6 he is known to have visited Venice, where he painted a great altarpiece for the church of S. Cassiano and worked on a number of portraits.

Antonello's painting lent impetus to two particular changes in Venetian art. Firstly, he speeded the development of oil as a painting medium in place of the traditional egg tempera; and in the wake of this transition to a more malleable medium came a completely new attitude to the use of light in the definition of form and detail. This new attitude to the control of light is so important that it deserves emphasis. A comparison of two Bellini *Madonnas* —perhaps fifteen years apart in date—will demonstrate the point. Both are superb paintings and show a skilful balance of colour, but in the earlier work the definition of the figures is largely achieved by a clear outline, whereas in the later one it is left very much to the play of light and shadow.

Once this discovery had been made, the way lay open to the incorporation of shadow tones into the colour scheme of the picture, and to the realisation that the whole range of any particular picture could be immeasurably enriched by the blending of light and dark tones in addition to the traditional blending of complementary colours. A spate of Antonellesque painting followed. The new understanding of shadow was used in the first instance to clarify structure by giving all lit surfaces a vivid intensity. This approach, applied to forms of architecture, schemes of landscape or details of costume, is typical not only of Giovanni Bellini at

this period but also of the generation of Cima da Conegliano and Alvise Vivarini. This style of painting was still ardently admired by the young Lorenzo Lotto in the opening years of the 16th century. Eventually the new discovery came to be used almost exclusively to enrich colour. The late paintings of Bellini are often remarkable not for the clarity of their structure, but for the depth of colour achieved by contrasting rich primary colours, lit by an intense light, with profound shadows.

LATE QUATTROCENTO VENETIAN PAINTING

Alongside these changes other developments occurred. During the years 1470–80 the Venetian *sacra conversazione* altarpiece took on the chief characteristics which it was to have for the next fifty years—a stately group of figures within a late 15th-century architectural setting. This convention was derived from Donatello's sculpture for the high altar of S. Antonio at Padua, but it was given a characteristic Venetian formality. One of the earliest examples is the S. Giobbe altarpiece of Giovanni Bellini himself.

Throughout this period Venetian artists maintained an almost late Gothic sensitivity to the beauties of the natural world. One of the earliest works of Giovanni Bellini sets St Jerome with his lion in a magical landscape reminiscent of the settings of early 15th-century artists such as Gentile da Fabriano. This feeling for landscape became a perma-

91. **Giovanni Bellini.** *The S. Giobbe altarpiece. c.* 1480. Paint on panel. 184¼ × 100½ in. (468 × 255 cm.). Accademia, Venice. The first great *sacra conversazione* of Venetian art to survive. The physical presence of the figures was originally emphasised by the wooden frame which was carved to correspond to the architectural setting of the painting. Their impressiveness is increased by the low viewpoint, by which means they seem to tower above the onlooker.

92. **Giorgione.** *La Tempesta. c.* 1503. Oil on canvas. 32¼ × 28¾ in. (82 × 73 cm.). Accademia, Venice. This is one of the few certain works by Giorgione and is one of the most famous early Renaissance landscapes. The subject of the work is uncertain and X-ray examination suggests that it may even have been changed in the course of painting. All that remains is a peculiarly evocative mood enhanced by the approaching storm in the background (compare plates 87 and 90).

nent feature of Venetian painting, and the landscape settings of Giovanni Bellini, Giorgione and Titian are famous. Yet those of less well known artists such as Lorenzo Lotto are no less striking—for instance, his painting of **91** *St Jerome in the Wilderness*, a work almost contemporary **92** with Giorgione's more famous *Tempesta*. The development of Venetian painting already mentioned had one particular effect on the Venetian representation of the countryside. Since the richest colouristic effects are to be found when the contrast between intense colour and shadow is at its greatest, Venetian painters came to favour the time of day most suited to these conditions. Thus, many scenes came to be set at those most evocative times, the hours around dawn and sunset, when intense sunlight is offset by deep shadows.

One further aspect of the Venetian tradition should be mentioned, namely the continued popularity enjoyed by a distinctive type of history painting or the painting of stories of both religious and secular subjects on a large scale. Elsewhere in Italy, large-scale interior paintings were generally executed in fresco, but in the course of the 15th century the Venetians discovered that paintings lasted longer in the sea air when painted on canvas. From *c.* 1480 onwards, therefore, it became customary to paint interior history paintings on huge areas of canvas mounted on a frame which was then installed in the required position. Throughout the later 15th and 16th centuries there was a constant demand by the republican government and the scuole for schemes

of decoration of this kind. The actual style of these paintings in the late 15th century had a certain amount in common with history paintings in Florence. Like a Ghirlandaio fresco, a late 15th-century Venetian history painting contains a great deal of incidental detail, portraits of important living people, and views of the home city. In Venice the style was based on the work of Jacopo Bellini, and of the surviving paintings the most remarkable are probably those of Carpaccio. He was no lover of dramatic action: even **93** when the most violent events are depicted, movement takes place but in suspended animation; and the senses are roused not by terror or awe at what is happening, but by the pleasing colour and the painter's detailed observation of the scene laid out before the eyes.

THE FONDACO DEI TEDESCHI

The first major monument of Venetian 16th-century art was the external decoration of the lately rebuilt Fondaco of the German merchants in 1507–8 by Giorgione and Titian. Like all external frescoes in Venice the originals soon perished, and the walls of the building now preserve only the faintest traces of paintings which had an impact in Venice similar to Michelangelo's *Bathers* cartoon in Florence. The arrangement of the decoration and the subject-matter can now only be approximately reconstructed from descriptions and a few engravings made in the 18th century. But we know that part of the decoration consisted of

93. **Vittore Carpaccio.** *A Miracle of the True Cross.* 1494–5. Oil on canvas. 143¾ × 153 in. (365 × 389 cm.). Accademia, Venice. Carpaccio was one of the great Venetian history painters on a grand scale. His style developed in the years around 1490 and emphasised the setting at the expense of the subject-matter (compare Ghirlandaio in Florence, plate 28). These settings are, however, superbly painted and present a vivid picture of Venetian life at this period.

94. *Nude female figure.* 1507–8. Engraving after Giorgione. Part of fresco decoration of the Fondaco dei Tedeschi, Venice. Very little is now known about the details of the decoration, almost all of which has vanished. The few fragments and literary descriptions suggest that the scheme included painted nude figures, seated and standing (as here), contained within an illusionistic architectural setting.

monumental figures set either in niches or in some other architectural context. It was probably this commission more than anything else which turned Venetian painters' minds to the problems connected with the painting of the human figure. The painters of the Fondaco were in part taking on the rôle of sculptors and, in its original state, the influence of the soft, reticent classicism of the Lombardi sculptors must have been apparent. The same dignity is to be found a little later in the superb paintings of female nude figures by Giorgione, Titian and Palma Vecchio.

94,92

The influence of the Lombardo family is to be seen also in the tendency at this time towards 'relief painting'. Whereas the narrative style of the Bellini family relied for its effect on enormous vistas in which the human element tended to be lost, the new generations of painters reduced this great expanse of setting by increasing the relative size of the figures and bringing them to the front of the picture space. The figures thus came to occupy the first attention of the onlooker. There are several instances of this in the early work of Titian, but the most exciting and revolutionary is certainly his enormous altarpiece of the *Assumption of the Virgin* painted for the Frari church in Venice (*c.* 1517). Perhaps basing his scheme on Mantegna's fresco of the same subject in the Eremitani church at Padua, Titian

95

emphatically arranged his apostles in a gesticulating mass across the panel, shutting out the background completely. The whole success of the painting rests on the actions and gestures of the figures which it contains.

With the *Assumption* the traditional decorum of Venetian painting was rudely shattered by the unprecedented excitement and vigour displayed. No satisfactory explanation of this sudden eruption has ever been found, but the *Assumption* is so alien to previous Venetian taste that Titian had presumably been inspired by some knowledge of works of art outside the city, perhaps of Roman origin.

CENTRAL ITALIAN ART AND VENICE: 1500–30

During this time the extraordinary flowering of art in Rome had already begun. The fame of artistic events at the papal court had already attracted away two promising young artists, Sebastiano del Piombo and Lorenzo Lotto, and, although no other notable Venetian artists travelled south at this time, a knowledge of events increasingly trickled north. The way in which developments outside Venice impinged on Venetian artists is part of the story that now has to be followed.

In architecture and sculpture the course of events is comparatively clear. The splendid creations of the Lombardi had not led to any spectacular developments either in architecture or in sculpture; and in both fields an undistinguished situation was relieved by the arrival of Jacopo Sansovino from Rome, after the Sack of 1527. It was he who built the first wholly classical buildings in Venice (including the library of S. Marco) and introduced the 82 sculptural style of Florence and Rome. Thence till his 85,101 death in 1570 his influence in these fields was paramount.

96. **Titian.** *St Sebastian. c.* 1520. Pen and ink with wash.
7 × 4½ in. (18 × 11·5 cm.). Städelsches Kunstinstitut, Frankfurt.
This study is connected with an altarpiece painted for a church
at Brescia. It is clearly based on the work of Michelangelo, and
in its Venetian context is a figure of unprecedented power and
vigour. It was not for another two decades, however, that Titian
attempted to develop this figure style.

97. *Façade of the Palazzo d'Anna*, Venice. *c.* 1535. Drawing after
Pordenone. 16¼ × 22 in. (41 × 56 cm.). Victoria and Albert
Museum, London. Pordenone was undoubtedly one of the most
talented and ingenious illusionistic painters of the first half of the
16th century. One of his most famous façade decorations was
that of the Palazzo d'Anna which fronted on the Grand Canal.
The figures which appear to leap and tumble into the canal and
the figure of a god flying in above are all typical products of
Pordenone's ingenious and inventive nature.

95. **Titian.** *Assumption of the Virgin.* 1516–18. Oil on panel.
27½ × 141¾ in. (690 × 360 cm.). Sta Maria Gloriosa dei Frari,
Venice. Titian may have been developing an idea first used by
Mantegna in the Eremitani chapel at Padua. In Venice the
vivid excitement of this work was without precedent and comes
as a considerable shock after the restraint of the
previous decades.

Jacopo Sansovino had been a friend of Bramante and Raphael. His figure style has great elegance and refinement, and it is perfectly understandable that it should have been acceptable to the Venetians. To begin with, at least, the work of Raphael and his followers exerted more influence than that of Michelangelo in the republic. The careful compositions and calculated delicacy of a painter such as Parmigianino presented a type of painting easily imposed on the reticent classicism of the first decade of the 16th century. Direct influence of Michelangelo's figure style is far harder to trace during the first forty years of the century and one particular instance illustrates well the type

96 of problem involved. This is the figure of St Sebastian from Titian's altarpiece now in the church of SS. Nazaro e Celso at Brescia. This figure is deliberately plagiarised from the two slaves executed during the second decade of the 16th century by Michelangelo for the Julius monument (they are now in the Louvre); and it is to be presumed that the vivid muscularity, the twisted limbs and the general expressiveness fascinated the young Titian. But the resulting figure is almost monstrously overweighted for its position in the Brescia polyptych, and by its mass and movement disturbs the balance of the whole altarpiece. Although it is known that the figure of St Sebastian had great admirers when it was painted (1520), it is without parallel in Titian's career until the 1540s.

PORDENONE

There was, however, one Venetian artist who was also much impressed by Michelangelo's work and who made strenuous attempts to master and to use its vivid actuality. This artist, Pordenone, had obscure origins in Friuli. It seems probable that he had some direct experience of Roman art but, apart from a general taste for struggling muscular figures derived from Michelangelo, he also quite suddenly developed an extreme and shocking style of illusionism. His main work is only on a large scale in fresco; and from the surfaces of domes, flat walls and external façades Pordenone bombarded the spectator with masses of swirling, tumbling, bulky figures. A good example of this was a palace façade overlooking the Grand Canal. Like the Fondaco dei Tedeschi, this perished after a comparatively short existence, but is, fortunately, known

97 through a drawing. Men and horses stumble out into the canal; a god flies in through an upper opening; the Roman hero Quintus Curtius, astride his charger, plunges outwards into the abyss. This façade was a very striking creation and it is not in the least surprising that Pordenone, if only by his shock tactics, acquired a reputation which, for a short time, rivalled that of Titian (Pordenone died in 1539).

THE PAINTING OF TITIAN FROM ABOUT 1540

During his lifetime Pordenone remained an isolated figure, but immediately after his death essays in the assimilation of Michelangelo's style became more frequent. The leading

figure continued to be Titian but at this point (*c.* 1540–50) the scene was joined by two considerably younger men, Tintoretto and Veronese. Titian's first successful surviving essay in this new figure style was a scheme of ceiling decoration for the church of S. Spirito in Isola, Venice (1542–3, now in Sta Maria della Salute). He may have been coaxed towards this style by a successful precedent of Pordenone, an illusionistic ceiling in the Doges' Palace which had strikingly foreshortened figures (now destroyed). One outstanding monument of this new figure style is the *St John the Baptist* from the church of Sta Maria Maggiore (now in the *98* Accademia, Venice). The strength and firmness of this statuesque figure are conveyed in subdued colouring, a feature common also to the ceiling paintings and other works of the period. The heaviness and plasticity were accompanied by a general reduction of the strength of the colouring, the overall tones tending to be dominated by blues, browns and greys.

This colouristic change in Titian's work was vitally important in the history of Venetian painting during the second half of the century; and it was accompanied by an equally important change in technique. Titian's working methods became broader and freer and the paint has greater fluidity. These changes have never been satisfactorily explained and perhaps they are best seen as the reaction of an ageing man (Titian was aged about 50) against a style which still had much in common with that of the early years of the century. Certainly at this point the vivid intense colouring common to Venetian artists, which with slight modifications had been in general usage since *c.* 1480, gives way to something more complex and frequently more sombre.

Since in its early stages the emphasis seems to have been on tone rather than colour, it is interesting that it was during these years that Titian painted his first known night scene (1548). The subject, the *Martyrdom of St Lawrence*, did not demand a night scene, but Titian used the subject as an essay in dark shadow, lit only by the flames of the fire, the surrounding torches and a beam of light from heaven. Thus all colouring was expunged from the scene, and the tonal unity of the work, based on the neutral colour of the shadow, is complete. For the next twenty years all Titian's works tended to have an individual tonal unity based on one or two particular colours. Within these limits the blending of complementary colours is often fantastically complicated but the final result is that every area of a picture has an equal strength. For example, forward areas and distant areas ceased to be differentiated in strength or type of colour.

The paintings in which this late style was developed included a number of mythological subjects, termed by Titian *poesie*, and commissioned by Philip II of Spain. The

(Continued on page 161)

THE VENETIAN RENAISSANCE

82. **Jacopo Sansovino.** *The Library of
S. Marco,* Venice. Begun 1537. This was
the first large High Renaissance building
in Venice, the façade being based on the
external wall of a Roman theatre.
Comparison with earlier buildings make
it easy to see how novel the classicism of
Sansovino was when it first appeared
in Venice.

83. **Vittore Carpaccio.** *View of the Doges'
Palace and S. Marco.* Detail of the painting
The Lion of St Mark. c. 1516. Paint on
canvas. Doges' Palace, Venice. The
façades of the chief palace in Venice date
from *c.* 1309–1424. It is built in an ornate
Gothic style and is partially faced in rose-
coloured marble. The impression of
colour was continued in the cathedral of
S. Marco behind, where mosaics played a
large part in the façade decoration.
Against these the order and discipline of
Sansovino's work (plate 82) appear very
striking.

84. **The Lombardo workshop.** *A
Miracle of St Mark. c.* 1490. Detail from
the façade of the Scuola di S. Marco,
Venice. Perhaps by Tullio Lombardo
(see figure 87) these reliefs show a strange
combination of a classical drapery style
with oriental turbans. The drapery is
characteristic of the period; unexpected is
the total treatment of the wall surface with
its illusionistic space. The emptiness of this
space and the concentration on the events
of the narrative portrayed contrast
strongly with the normal approach of
contemporary painters (see figure 93).

85. **Jacopo Sansovino.** *Hermes.*
c. 1537–40. Bronze. h. 58½ in. (149 cm.).
Loggetta di S. Marco, Venice. Jacopo
Sansovino, the heir of Bramante as an
architect, was the heir of Raphael as a
figure sculptor. The four figures on the
Loggetta combine with the architecture
to form one of the most accomplished and
elegant compositions in Venice. Jacopo
Sansovino was the first High Renaissance
sculptor in Venice.

86. **Antonello da Messina.**
Il Condottiere. Dated 1475. Paint on panel.
13¾ × 11 in. (35 × 28 cm.). Louvre,
Paris. Antonello was one of the most
influential outsiders ever to visit Venice.
The effect of his work can be gauged from
plates 88 and 89. One of his most important types of painting was the portrait,
where his use of light rather than line to
define form and detail is particularly
striking.

87. **Lorenzo Lotto.** *Portrait. c.* 1506–8.
Paint on panel. 16½ × 14 in. (42·3 × 35·8
cm.). Kunsthistorisches Museum, Vienna.
The effects of Antonello's style were still
being felt in the early 16th century. Lotto,
one of the most gifted of the young
generation of Venetian artists, gave his
portraits the brilliance and directness
made popular by Antonello.

88. **Giovanni Bellini.** *Madonna and Child.*
c. 1465. Paint on panel, transferred to
canvas. 20½ × 17 in. (52 × 42·5 cm.).
Correr Museum, Venice. When Giovanni
Bellini painted this *Madonna and Child*
he was still strongly influenced by the
style of his brother-in-law Andrea
Mantegna. The painting of the Child, for
instance, is dry and linear and the folds
of the drapery are hard and clear. The
colouring is, however, gentle and the
blending of different shades of red
extremely delicate.

89. **Giovanni Bellini.** *Madonna and Child.*
c. 1480. Paint on panel. $25\frac{1}{2} \times 19$ in.
(65 × 48 cm.). Burrell Collection,
Glasgow Art Gallery and Museum.
The change in style since the date

of plate 88 is most easily seen in the
treatment and use of light. It is noticeable
that the background is screened by a
curtain so that the light source can be
controlled. It is interesting that at about

the same time, similar experiments were
being made by the young Leonardo in
Florence. Here, in Venice, the impetus
seems to have come from Antonello da
Messina (see plate 86).

IHOVANES BELINVS

VENETIAN LANDSCAPE PAINTING

90. **Giovanni Bellini.** *St Jerome in the Wilderness. c.* 1460. Tempera on panel. 17¾ × 14 in. (45 × 35·5 cm.). Barber Institute of Fine Art, University of Birmingham. One of Giovanni Bellini's earliest undated works and closely related to the drawings of his father, Jacopo. The sensitivity of the landscape and the radiance of its lighting and colouring are part of an older tradition which can be seen at work in the painting of Gentile da Fabriano.

91. **Lorenzo Lotto.** *St Jerome in the Wilderness. c.* 1506. Paint on panel. 18¾ × 15¾ in. (48 × 40 cm.). Louvre, Paris. The evocative character of Venetian landscape painting is famous (see also plate 92) and was greatly enhanced by the new insight into the use of light derived from the work of Antonello. Giorgione's *Tempesta* (figure 92) is the most famous example of the early 16th century, but this small panel of Lotto is hardly less creative with its suggestion of barren solitude.

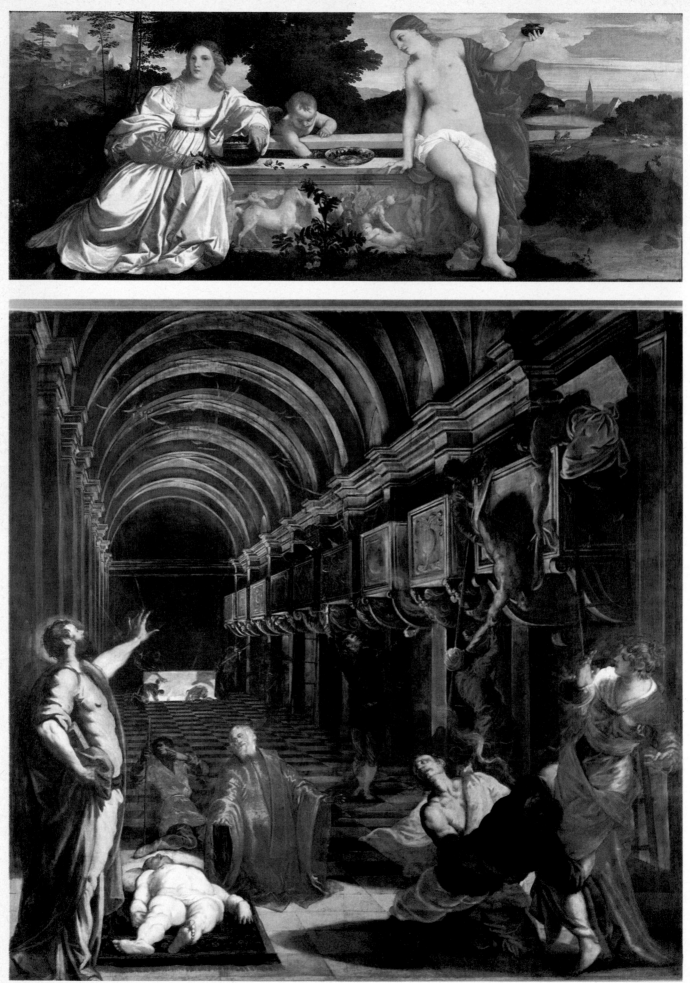

92. **Tiziano Vecelli (Titian).** *Sacred and Profane Love. c.* 1515. Paint on canvas. 46¾ × 111 in. (118 × 282 cm.). Borghese Gallery, Rome. Perhaps the most famous, although not the first female studies of the Venetian High Renaissance. The relief-like composition is notable, set against a remarkable romantic landscape.

93. **Jacopo Robusti (Tintoretto).** *The Finding of the Body of St Mark. c.* 1562. Paint on canvas. 159½ × 159½ in. 405·2 × 405·2 cm.). Brera, Milan. Originally in the Scuola di S. Marco, this belongs to the same class of painting as much of the work of Carpaccio. The concentration of dramatic interest which has taken place is clear. Note also Tintoretto's dramatic use of light.

94. **Paolo Caliari (Veronese).** *The Mystic Marriage of St Catherine. c.* 1560. 148½ × 95¼ in. (377 × 242 cm.). Accademia, Venice. One of Veronese's most sumptuous altarpieces, this painting is in sharp contrast to the work of Tintoretto. Veronese's love of bright colours, costume and beautiful architecture link him with the earlier tradition of Carpaccio and Gentile Bellini.

95. **Titian.** *Perseus and Andromeda. c.* 1560.
Paint on canvas. 70½ × 77¾ in.
(179 × 197·5 cm.). Wallace Collection,
London. One of a group of works dis-
patched to Philip II of Spain. Comparison with plate 92 will show the
intervening change in Titian's style. The
painting is given a general colour tone
which unites all parts of the work. The
figure elements of the narrative became
shapes within this colour construction.

96. **Tintoretto.** *The Ascension.*
c. 1576–81. Paint on canvas. 211¾ × 128
in. (538 × 325 cm.). Scuola di
S. Rocco, Venice. Part of Tintoretto's
most famous undertaking (see figure 99),
this makes an interesting comparison with
the earlier work of Titian (plate 95).
Both artists have a fully mastered figure
style and both use figures as shapes to be
disposed within a surface pattern with
only a secondary regard for depth.
Tintoretto's result is consciously extravagant and dramatic, with its extremes of
brilliance and shadow and sudden changes
of figure scale.

97. **Titian.** *Ippolito de' Medici* (detail).
c. 1533. Paint on canvas. $54\frac{1}{4} \times 41\frac{3}{4}$ in.
(138×106 cm.). Pitti Palace, Florence.
Part of one of the portraits from Titian's
middle period. The costume, so important
in this type of portrait, is said to be
Hungarian, recording a military expedi-
tion of Ippolito. The image is proud,
arrogant and withdrawn and must surely
have been very flattering to the sitter.

98. **Lorenzo Lotto.** *Andrea Odoni.*
Signed and dated 1527. Paint on canvas.
$44\frac{3}{4} \times 39\frac{3}{4}$ in. (114×101 cm.). Royal
Collection, Hampton Court. Unlike the
portraits of Titian, up to *c.* 1540, Lotto's
are seldom reserved or withdrawn. Here
the well known collector, Odoni, offers
part of his collection to the spectator for
inspection.

99. **Titian.** *Pope Paul III with his Nephews Alessandro and Ottavio. c.* 1546. Paint on canvas. 83 × 68¾ in. (200 × 127 cm.). Galleria Nazionale di Capodimonte, Naples. One of the most extraordinary pieces of artistic licence in art history, in which a senile pope turns towards an obsequious nephew. Large areas of drapery were never finished and it has been conjectured that the Farnese family objected to the work. This style of portraiture is a long way from the flattery accorded to Ippolito de Medici (see plate 97).

100. **Jacopo da Ponte (Bassano).**
Pastoral Scene. Paint on canvas. $54\frac{1}{2} \times 50\frac{1}{4}$
in. ($138\cdot5 \times 127\cdot5$ cm.). Thyssen-Bornemisza Collection, Switzerland. Jacopo
Bassano lived most of his life at Bassano.
His style was closely linked to the
metropolitan style of Venice, and his
characteristic works of pastoral subjects,
painted in dark tones with brilliant white
lights, date from the 1550s onwards.

series, now scattered among numerous collections, illustrates the full range of Titian's development between 1550 and 1560 and demonstrates in addition how he finally absorbed the contrasted figure styles of Michelangelo and Raphael's followers (particularly Parmigianino).

PORTRAITS

During the years in which these major changes were taking place in Titian's figure style and approach to colour, it is not surprising that other changes are apparent, particularly in his portraiture. Titian from his earliest years was a brilliant portraitist and his work quickly became fashionable among the Italian princes. A typical portrait of the

97 1530s, that of the cardinal Ippolito de' Medici in Hungarian costume, shows a proud self-assured aristocrat in richly coloured clothing—a picture of the cardinal as he undoubtedly would have liked to see himself. This attitude to his sitters Titian replaced during the 1540s by a more personal interpretation of the subject seated in front of him. The climax of this was the unfinished triple portrait of

99 Pope Paul III and his two nephews. The seated pope is shown as a senile old man attended by two shifty and obsequious relatives. In general Titian's portraits of the 1540s are among his most powerful and penetrating creations. They include two contrasted studies of his friend Pietro Aretino and a number of other portraits painted in Rome and during his visits to the imperial court at Augsburg. Of all these the portrait with the most important influence was his equestrian study of Charles V; indeed centuries of subsequent equestrian portraiture have perhaps obscured the curiously personal character of this vision of the ageing emperor galloping in full armour through the totally deserted and utterly romantic landscape of the Veneto.

Lack of space has made it impossible to deal adequately with Italian portraiture. Its introduction at this stage does not mean that Venetian portraiture determined the course of portraiture in the remainder of Italy. Unquestionably the most influential portraitist during the first twenty years of the century was Raphael. Titian, who imitated Raphael prototypes in his portraits of Paul III and his Farnese nephews, was not alone in following Raphael's lead. Raphael set new standards for court portraiture and much of the subsequent development of portraiture in Italy followed indications already suggested by him. Alongside Titian there existed a considerable number of other Italian portrait painters, many of whom have already been mentioned in other contexts—Rosso Fiorentino, Pontormo, Parmigianino, Bronzino and Salviati among them. Indeed in Venice itself other talented portrait painters were also active; and although Titian alone had an international reputation the more intimate personal style of Lorenzo Lotto and Palma Vecchio is worth mentioning. A painter of inspired technique but unpredictable invention, Lorenzo

91 Lotto achieved some of his greatest results in this type of work.

98. **Titian.** *St John the Baptist* (detail). *c.* 1542. Oil on canvas. 79 × 52¾ in. (201 × 134 cm.). Accademia, Venice. Formerly in Sta Maria Maggiore. Perhaps Titian's greatest essay in a Michelangelesque figure style. The calm gesture and noble proportions are extremely impressive. This work forms part of a general change in the Venetian painters' attitude towards figure painting and their general acceptance of many of the characteristics of central Italian art.

99. *The Upper Hall*, the Scuola di S. Rocco, Venice. The Scuola was built between 1517 and *c.* 1545. The painted decoration of the interior is entirely by Tintoretto who worked there spasmodically from 1564 up to 1587. The Upper Hall was decorated 1576–81. This Scuola is the only one to survive with its decorative schemes intact, illustrating the splendour and sumptuousness of Venetian public buildings. It is remarkable how well the flashing colour of Tintoretto's canvases blends with the heavy gilded woodwork of the ceiling.

TINTORETTO

In the whole field of Venetian painting the years around 1545 saw fundamental changes. In 1548 a newcomer made his first public appearance in a painting for the Scuola di S. Marco. His name was Jacopo Robusti, called Tintoretto; and the painting was of one of the miracles of St Mark, *The Miracle of the Slave*. From the outset Tintoretto committed himself to a dramatic and bold style in which his main intention was generally to force the spectator into some form of subjective emotional involvement. To this end all means were used including lighting and shadow, and an emphasis on the human figure unprecedented in Venetian art apart from the works of Titian of the 1540s, as we have seen. Tintoretto's earliest biographer, Ridolfi, writing in the next century, related both how he admired Michelangelo and how he was accustomed to experiment with lighting by using miniature stage sets inside boxes, in which the lighting could be controlled. Tintoretto was also said to have studied the human figure from unexpected angles by suspending small clay models in the air. Naturally the results of these experiments do not all suddenly appear in the same painting; but the theatrical nature of another work for the Scuola di S. Marco, *The Finding of the Body of St Mark*, must surely have resulted from such experiments.

Tintoretto had very little use for settings as objects of intrinsic interest, thus dividing himself from a recurrent feature of the Venetian pictorial tradition. Settings are the 'outer casings' designed to contain the drama within. Indeed throughout much of his greatest work, the decoration of the Scuola di S. Rocco, interest in the natural or architectural settings is extremely perfunctory. Space as a compositional device is almost eliminated, the constant tendency being to arrange the figures in a strong pattern across the surface of the canvas, regardless of their presumed depth in space. Titian had already gone some way towards this conception in his *poesie*, but on the whole Tintoretto's colouring—perhaps influenced by the dark tonality of some of Titian's work—has none of the gentleness of the *poesie*. Tintoretto's technique of contrasting areas of deep shadow with intense colour may have been designed for the physical setting in which his canvases were to be placed—a setting of dark wooden panelling relieved only by ornate carving and ponderous gilding. Certainly the deep shadows of Tintoretto's painting blend perfectly with this framework, while the coloured shapes take up the decorative rhythms of the gilded wood-carving. The work is divided between three rooms, and in the main room on the first floor Tintoretto's approach to space becomes most arbitrary. Thus he juxtaposes tiny distant figures and enormous foreground figures, a device which discourages any attempted spatial comprehension by the spectator.

93

96

99

100. *The main salon, Villa Barbaro*, Maser, near Castelfranco. Built by Palladio; decorated by Veronese *c.* 1559–60. Veronese's feeling for beautiful architecture is well illustrated by the painted architecture of this cruciform room. Through the painted arches are seen fantastic painted landscapes so that within the house one is constantly reminded of the purpose of a villa as a country retreat.

101. **Jacopo Sansovino.** *Neptune.* 1554–67. Doges' Palace, Venice. The pair of figures of which this is one were among the earliest gigantic statues to be executed in Venice. To this extent Venice lagged behind Florence where the taste for colossal nude figures went back at least as far as the *David* of Michelangelo (see figure 45). Sansovino's touch is visible in the closely contained outlines and movement of the figure.

VERONESE

Tintoretto was, in a sense, a history painter first and a decorator second. There is little sensuous enjoyment to be felt in front of most of his painting because the subject-matter was so intensely felt and portrayed by the artist. The decorative quality of these S. Rocco paintings is of a highly specialised kind, as though Tintoretto had forced his intensely dramatic style into a decorative role. However, at the same time in Venice there lived another major artist whose work is so consciously decorative that dramatic action is either avoided or is so artificial as to be unbelievable. This artist was Paolo Veronese, who at the age of about twenty was already engaged in the decoration of villas and country houses. Regardless of the subject on which he was engaged, his work always remained that of a decorator at the highest level of genius. In almost every respect his painting differed from that of Tintoretto. He painted many large and brilliant altarpieces, a type of work to which Tintoretto was seldom attracted. He avoided scenes of emotional or dramatic content and will almost certainly be remembered for his series of 'supper scenes' (*The Last Supper, Christ in the House of the Pharisee* and others) in which a magnificent architectural setting is filled out with all the paraphernalia of a rich man's household —servants, friends, animals, guards and so on.

Unlike Tintoretto, Veronese dwelt lovingly on architec-

tural detail. He often worked in collaboration with architects such as Michele Sanmicheli of Verona, or Andrea Palladio; and one of his greatest decorative schemes was the interior decoration of the Palladian Villa Barbaro at Maser (near Castelfranco). Here his appreciation of beautiful architecture was given full play because much of decoration consists of a painted architectural scheme superimposed on the plain bare wall-surfaces of the rooms. *100*

Veronese's emphasis on detail strongly recalls the history paintings of the Bellini and Carpaccio; although the figure style is totally different, the range of interests is similar enough to suspect that both artists catered for a permanent aspect of Venetian taste. There is a further affinity in colouring. Unlike the mellow tones of Carpaccio's work, Veronese's painting has a silvery appearance. But both laid great emphasis on colour itself in dress and costume as a decorative element; and for Veronese the deep shadows common in Tintoretto's style were not allowed to intrude and to destroy this festive and brilliant impression.

BASSANO

Of the many secondary painters belonging to this Venetian tradition, one of the most interesting is Jacopo da Ponte, who is generally known, after his home town, as Bassano. He lived a large part of his life there; but he was trained in

94

102. **Alessandro Vittoria.** *St Jerome.* Before 1568. Marble. h. 75½ in. (192 cm.). Sta Maria Gloriosa dei Frari, Venice. Part of an altar erected by the Zane family, of which large parts have since been destroyed. The composition of this figure is such that it can never have blended with any architecture but must always have appeared as a violent actor on a stage.

Venice (*c.* 1530) in the workshop of a lesser artist Bonifazio de' Pitati and during the course of a long life (he died in 1592) the series of major changes in his style always reflected artistic ideas current in Venice. Thus, a style modelled on Bonifazio was succeeded *c.* 1540 by a stylistic phase much influenced by Pordenone; and it was only after this (during the 1550s) that he began to paint in his more familiar manner with dark tones offset by brilliant white highlights and flashes of radiant colour (certainly under the influence of his contemporary, Tintoretto). What might have been an undistinguished provincial career was relieved by the production of a large number of paintings of a particular kind—those scenes of rustic life linked loosely to a Biblical subject, with which Bassano's name is now generally associated. These detailed paintings of peasants, animals, fruit, vegetables and other rustic objects, distantly reminiscent of the contemporary work of Breughel, were unusual and made Bassano famous in his own day. Already by the 1560s they were becoming collector's pieces.

VITTORIA

The change which overtook Venetian painting during the 1540s also affected sculpture. The Venetians developed a taste for colossal statuary and, following the commission of a statue of *Neptune* for the Piazza S. Marco (*c.* 1544, lost),

the Venetian senate commissioned Jacopo Sansovino to carve two great figures representing *Mars* and *Neptune* for the Doges' Palace (1554). Standing on the main staircase in the courtyard of the palace, these figures are very impressive. They show that Sansovino still exercised the closest control over his compositions, even on an heroic scale and in a commission free of architectural restraint. The figures have a closely contained silhouette, and it is this compact nature and the frontality of their poses which produces their dramatic impact on the spectator.

Jacopo Sansovino was accustomed to employ a large number of assistants. Buildings such as the library of S. Marco were intended to be decorated by quantities of figure sculpture which Sansovino, as a matter of course, left to his assistants. One such assistant was Alessandro Vittoria, a sculptor from Trento who arrived in Venice in 1543 and was destined to become the most distinguished sculptor working in Venice during the second half of the century. To call him a pupil of Sansovino would be misleading; they certainly quarrelled, and the young Vittoria, about 40 years junior to Sansovino, found his true inspiration in the work of Michelangelo. His style was opposed in many ways to Sansovino's, and the sources of his inspiration are to be sought in the sculpture of the Julius II monument rather than the Loggetta or the Doges' Palace. In particular the Michelangelo *Slaves* seem perpetually to have fascinated Vittoria. These, it will be recalled, had been known to Titian as early as 1520 while he was working on the Brescia altarpiece; but there the *St Sebastian* had been an isolated essay in a Michelangelesque style. Vittoria constantly returned to the contrasted compositions of the two *Slaves*, and these influenced the form which several of his most notable works were to take. It is not therefore surprising that his style of sculpture is very different from that of Sansovino; sculpture for Vittoria was not something to be contained within the main outlines of its architectural setting. Instead, in a manner similar to Michelangelo's intentions for the sculpture of the Julius II monument, his statues move in front of the architecture with a vigour and freedom, setting up rhythms which are frequently in contrast to their setting.

16TH-CENTURY ARCHITECTURE IN THE VENETO

Jacopo Sansovino and the Veronese Michele Sanmicheli, two of the most important 16th-century architects working in the region controlled by Venice, came north after the Sack of Rome in 1527. Both had spent many years there and both were completely familiar with the architecture of Bramante and his successors. In some sense the architecture of both formed a commentary on that of Bramante for, like Raphael, both showed in different ways how the austerity of Bramante's work might be enriched and enlivened. Amongst other work in Verona, Sanmicheli designed three palaces, each of which is based on the design of the Casa di Raffaello in Rome. But in each the architectural decoration is significantly varied and augmented.

This increased surface richness is also to be found in the work of Sansovino. His most notable Venetian building, the library of S. Marco (begun 1537), is not based immediately on any building by Bramante; the tiers of arcading are closer to the Roman Theatre of Marcellus. But the amount of carved decoration is striking; and the carved swags of flowers and fruit along the upper frieze are reminiscent of the stucco decoration on Raphael's Palazzo dell'Aquila. Nevertheless, although Sansovino was an ingenious manipulator of classical architectural motifs and decorative ideas, his architecture retains an august three-dimensional gravity.

Of all later 16th-century Italian architects Andrea Palladio was probably the most influential. For in 1570 he published *Li Quattro Libri dell' Architettura*, a work which is more scholarly and extensive than any other 16th-century Italian treatise on architecture; but besides Palladio's ideas they also contained his original work, for most of the buildings for which he was responsible are illustrated. In his youth he visited Rome in the company of a humanist called Trissino, and there in 1540–1 made a thorough study of the antique remains. However, most of his life was spent in Vicenza where much of his work is to be found. He also worked in Venice, and the church of S. Giorgio Maggiore, set on its island opposite the Doges' Palace, is probably his most familiar building.

Palladio drew upon a wide variety of sources. He admired the symmetry and order of Bramante's work but, after the manner of Bramante's successors, his work is carefully enlivened by a limited amount of sculptural decorations. As a whole his work was so judiciously balanced and consistent that it still appeals to architects.

Palladio's fame rests also on his splendid series of villas. The villa, as an architectural commission, was a comparatively recent arrival on the scene. The idea of the villa was certainly publicised by Alberti in the 15th century, but the actual building of villas depended on the realisation of patrons that it was now possible to have a country retreat which was not also a fortified castle. In the years around 1480 the Medici family built the famous villa at Poggio a Caiano which must have been among the earliest buildings of this type. Nevertheless there were different types of country retreat: some, like the Palazzo del Tè, were very close to the city; others, built at a considerable distance, were based on family farm property for the supply of provisions and necessities. Palladio constructed both, but the majority belong to the second, more rural, variety. Both Sansovino and Sanmicheli had designed villas; and it was from the Villa Soranza of Sanmicheli (1545–55, destroyed) that Palladio took one of his most characteristic ideas, that of building projecting wings stretching out from the main block. These wings were normally used to connect the main block with the outbuildings; but subjectively they seem to reach out and to embrace the countryside in which the building stands.

The formal satisfaction given by Palladio's villas derives chiefly from their symmetry. This is often aided by the placing of a classical portico with columns and pediment across the main front of the central block. Once, in the Villa Rotonda, Vicenza, the idea was repeated on all four sides of the house, giving an effect of complete symmetry and perfect balance. The classical portico perhaps gives his villas the appearance of timeless grandeur and elegance; it was certainly the feature most frequently exploited by the Palladian imitators of 18th-century England.

CONCLUSION

The 16th century was the century not merely of the Renaissance but also of the Reformation. Some mention has already been made of the Counter-Reformation and its effects on art. These effects were real in Italy, particularly in art associated with the Society of Jesus (founded 1540). It may be asked, therefore, whether the Reformation had comparable effects. But the nature of the various religious movements which made up the Reformation was such that its effects were totally different. The decrees of the Council of Trent which embody much of the essence of the Counter-Reformation were at least concerned with the reform of the content of ecclesiastical art rather than its destruction. But the reformed Churches of Luther and Calvin found themselves against so much of the very content of traditional religious art that they had no option but to destroy it. Thus many forms of art connected with religious observance —for instance, altarpieces, stained glass or carved images— ceased to be required altogether in those areas which in the 16th century came ecclesiastically to be controlled by a reformed Church. This, however, merely produced the negative result that artists had to make a living from those secular branches of their profession which were still permissible. It was still possible to paint portraits and genre paintings, to carve garden decorations and public monuments and to build palaces and town halls.

Some artists are known to have had reformist sympathies or to have been in touch with men of known reformist sympathies. This applies to many of the great northern painters *c.* 1525 and includes such men of widely differing styles as Dürer who, in spite of his appointment as court painter to the emperor, knew Luther and was also a friend of Erasmus, Holbein who lived much of his life at the Protestant court of England and also knew Erasmus, Cranach, court painter at the Protestant court of Saxony, and Grünewald who appears to have had Lutheran inclinations. Yet there seems little common ground between these artists to suggest 'Reformation characteristics'; and while the painting of Grünewald may seem to suggest psychological disturbance, there is nothing to prove that this disturbance can be interpreted directly as a 'sign of the times'.

Many writers have tried to summarise the character of the Renaissance world. In art, the changes may be seen as an abandonment of a Gothic style and a transition to one based on antique precedent. Many great changes can

103. **Michele Sanmicheli.** *Palazzo Bevilacqua*, Verona. *c.* 1530.
The design of this palace was based on Sanmicheli's recent
Roman experience, particularly the Casa di Rafaello
(see figure 54). Sanmicheli has, however, varied the ornament
considerably, adding embellishments to suit his own taste and
possibly that of a client who wished for a more sumptuous
appearance.

104. **Andrea Palladio.** *Villa Barbaro*, Maser, near
Castelfranco. *c.* 1550–60. This is perhaps Palladio's most serene
and successful country villa. The wings of the plan (which
actually contain out-houses) seem to stretch out to embrace the
countryside. Inside (see figure 101) one is continually reminded
of the presence of the countryside and of the open air through
the fresco decorations of Veronese.

be seen in other fields of human activity; indeed, if any
particular period of history merits the title 'transitional'
more than any other period, the 15th and 16th centuries
must have a high claim to consideration. The consolidation
of new nation states in France and England, the ultimate
feebleness of the Holy Roman Empire as an effective
political institution; the religious protest of Luther, the
growth of Protestantism and the disappearance of a
Universal Church; the geographical discoveries of the
Portuguese and Spaniards; the astronomical theories of
Copernicus and Galileo—all these fall within the years
1400–1600 and run parallel to the re-evaluation of the
culture of classical antiquity.

The main subject of this book has been the 'classical
revival'. Of this expression, the word 'revival' is worth
emphasis since this was a new element in Western art. In
discussing the impact of Italian art on the North, it was
suggested that one of the advantages of Italian art was that
it had a specious semblance of 'rightness' when compared
with other styles. This was almost entirely due to the fact
that it was essentially a revivalist style with an august body
of literature and monuments as a court of appeal to back it.
Not all the genius of Michelangelo, Raphael and Bramante
can hide this aspect of the Italian Renaissance. The spread
of classicism committed Europe to three hundred years of
revivalism in art from which it only began to emerge at the
end of the last century. Whether this was good or bad is
obviously immaterial; it happened, it was a new phenomenon, and it emerged within the period covered by this book.

The years around 1400 had a certain convenience as a
beginning to this book since the pervasive International
Gothic style provided some sort of common point of
departure for European art. It would be extremely difficult
and indeed rash to attempt to present as tidy a picture of
art in 1575. No comparable state of affairs existed. For
whereas by 1730 most European countries had devised a
classicising idiom of their own which gave a semblance of
unity to European art comparable with that which it had
possessed in the 14th century, in the 16th century this was
still very far from being the case. It is at this point, therefore, that the reader must pass on to the 17th century.

Further Reading List

GENERAL EUROPEAN ART AND HISTORY

Gombrich, E. H. *The Story of Art*, revised ed. 1964 (Phaidon)

Holt, E. G. (ed.) *A Documentary History of Art*, 2 vols, 1958 (Doubleday Anchor Books)

Panofsky, E. *Renaissance and Renascences in Western Art* (Humanities Press)

Pevsner, N. *An Outline of European Architecture*, enlarged ed. 1960 (Penguin Books)

ITALIAN ART AND HISTORY
General background

Burckhardt, J. *The Civilisation of the Renaissance in Italy*, various English editions

Castiglione, B. *The Book of the Courtier*, 1959 (Dent)

Cellini, B. *Autobiography*, various English editions

Gragg, F. A. (tr.) *Memoirs of a Renaissance Pope* (Pius II), 1960 (Allen and Unwin)

Hay, D. *The Italian Renaissance in its Historical Background*, 1961 (Cambridge U.P.)

Landucci, Luca *A Florentine Diary from 1450 to 1516*, 1927 (Dent)

Machiavelli, N. *The Prince*, various English editions

Mattingly, G. *Renaissance Diplomacy*, 1963 (Penguin Books)

Vespasiano *The Vespasiano Memoirs* (Vespasiano da Bisticci), 1963 (Harper and Row)

Sources on Art

Alberti, L. B. *On Painting*, 1st ed. 1435, English tr. 1956 (Yale U.P.)

Alberti, L. B. *Ten Books on Architecture*, 1st ed. 1485, English tr. 1726, reprinted 1955 (Tiranti; Transatlantic Arts)

Ghiberti, L. *Commentarii*, 1st ed. *c.* 1450 (ed. Schlosser, Berlin 1912, in Italian and German. No complete English translation yet exists; extracts in Holt, see above)

Vasari, G. *Lives of the Architects, Painters and Sculptors*, 1st ed. 1550, 2nd enlarged ed. 1568 of which various English editions

General Works on Art

Berenson, B. *Italian Pictures of the Renaissance: The Florentine School*, 2 vols, 1963 (Phaidon)

Berenson, B. *Italian Pictures of the Renaissance: The Venetian School*, 2 vols, 1957 (Phaidon)

Blunt, A. *Artistic Theory in Italy 1450–1600*, new ed. 1956 (Oxford U.P.)

Briganti, G. *Italian Mannerism* (Van Nostrand 1962; Thames and Hudson 1963)

Freedberg, S. J. *Painting of the High Renaissance in Rome and Florence*, 2 vols, 1961 (Harvard U.P.)

Hennessy, J. Pope *Italian Gothic Sculpture*, 1955 (Phaidon)

Hennessy, J. Pope *Italian High Renaissance and Baroque Sculpture*, 3 vols, 1963 (Phaidon)

Hennessy, J. Pope *Italian Renaissance Sculpture*, 1958 (Phaidon)

Marle, R. van *The Development of the Italian Schools of Painting*, 19 vols, 1923–38 (Martinus Nijhoff, The Hague)

Murray, P. *The Architecture of the Italian Renaissance* (Batsford 1963; Schocken 1964)

Wittkower, R. *Architectural Principles in the Age of Humanism*, 1949 (Tiranti; Random House)

Monographs

Berti, L. *Masaccio*, 1964 (Istituto Editoriale Italiano, Milan, in Italian)

Clark, K. *Leonardo da Vinci*, 1939 (Cambridge U.P.)

Crowe, J. A., and Cavalcaselle, G. B. *Titian: His Life and Times*, 2 vols, 1881 (John Murray)

Hendy, P., and Goldscheider, L. *Giovanni Bellini*, 1945 (Phaidon)

Janson, H. W. *The Sculpture of Donatello*, 2nd ed. 1963 (Princeton U.P.)

Krautheimer, R., and Hess, T. K. *Lorenzo Ghiberti*, 1956 (Princeton U.P.)

Kristeller, P. *Andrea Mantegna*, 1901 (Longmans, Green)

Richter, G. M. *Giorgio da Castelfranco, called Giorgione*, 1937 (Chicago U.P.)

Suida, W. E. *Raphael*, 1941 (Phaidon)

Tolnay, C. de *Michelangelo*, several vols, from 1943 (Princeton U.P.)

Various authors 'Library of World Art' series, from 1961 (Oldbourne Press)

EUROPE OUTSIDE ITALY—ART AND HISTORY
General background

Cartellieri, O. *The Court of Burgundy: studies in the history of civilisation*, 1929 (London)

Huizinga, J. *The Waning of the Middle Ages*, 1924 (Penguin Books; Doubleday Anchor Books)

General Works on Art

Benesch, O. *The Art of the Renaissance in Northern Europe*, 1965 (Phaidon)

Blunt, A. *Art and Architecture in France, 1500–1700*, 1953 (Penguin Books, Pelican History of Art)

Frankl, P. *Gothic Architecture*, 1962 (Penguin Books, Pelican History of Art)

Friedländer, M. J. *From Van Eyck to Bruegel*, 1956 (Phaidon)

Matějček, A., and Pešina, J. *Gothic Painting in Bohemia 1350–1450*, 1956 (Artia, Prague)

Muller, P. H. A. *Sculpture in the Netherlands, Germany, France and Spain 1400–1500*, 1966 (Penguin Books, Pelican History of Art)

Müller, T. *Deutsche Plastik der Renaissance*, 1963 (Langewiesche, Königstein im Taunus)

Panofsky, E. *Early Netherlandish Painting*, 1953 (Harvard U.P.)

Porcher, J. *French Miniatures from Illuminated Manuscripts*, 1960 (Collins)

Ring, G. *A Century of French Painting, 1400–1500*, 1949 (Phaidon)

Summerson, J. *Architecture in Britain, 1530–1830*, 1963 (Penguin Books, Pelican History of Art)

Webb, G. *Architecture in Britain: The Middle Ages*, 1950 (Penguin Books, Pelican History of Art)

Monographs

Baldass, L. *Jan van Eyck*, 1952 (Phaidon)

Beenken, H. *Rogier van der Weyden*, 1951 (Munich, in German)

Gerstenberg, K. *Tilman Riemenschneider*, 3rd ed. 1950 (F. Bruckmann, Munich, in German)

Lutze, E. *Veit Stoss*, 1952 (Deutscher Kunstverlag, Munich, in German)

Panofsky, E. *The Life and Art of Albrecht Dürer*, 1955 (Princeton U.P.)

Troescher, G. *Claus Sluter*, 1951 (Paris, in German)

Wertheimer, O. *Nicolaus Gerhaert*, 1929 (Berlin, in German)

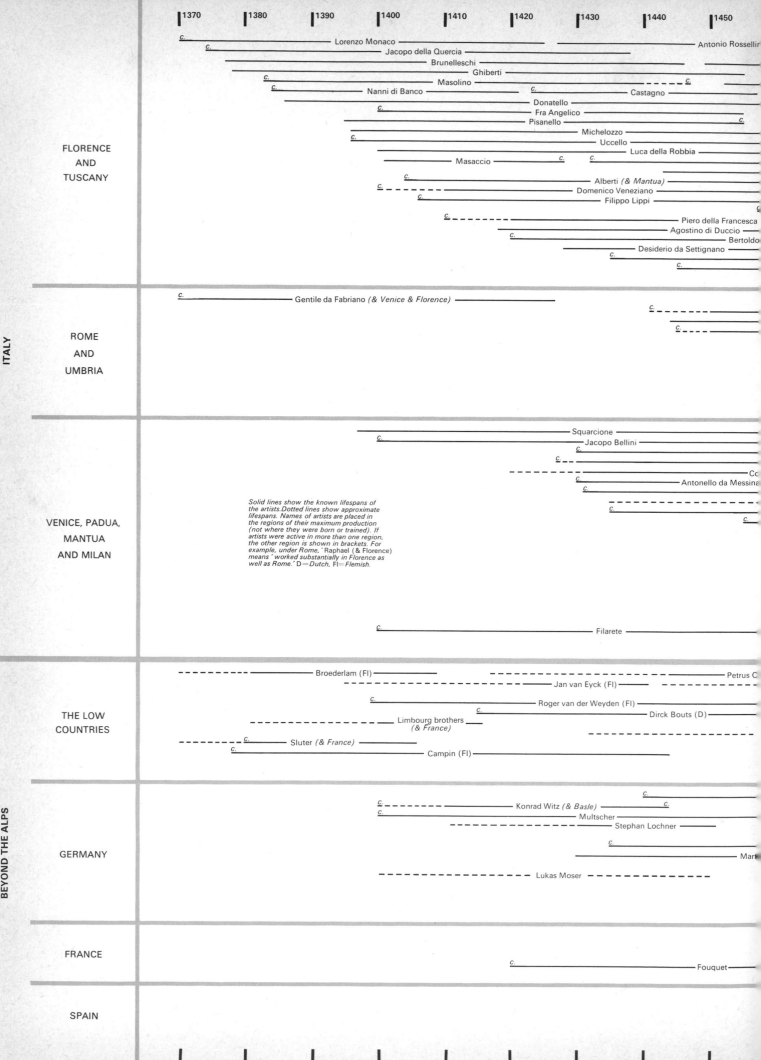

ITALY

FLORENCE AND TUSCANY

Lorenzo Monaco — Antonio Rossellino
Jacopo della Quercia
Brunelleschi
Ghiberti
Masolino
Nanni di Banco — Castagno
Donatello
Fra Angelico
Pisanello
Michelozzo
Uccello
Luca della Robbia
Masaccio
Alberti *(& Mantua)*
Domenico Veneziano
Filippo Lippi
Piero della Francesca
Agostino di Duccio
Bertoldo
Desiderio da Settignano

ROME AND UMBRIA

Gentile da Fabriano *(& Venice & Florence)*

VENICE, PADUA, MANTUA AND MILAN

Squarcione
Jacopo Bellini
Co
Antonello da Messina
Filarete

Solid lines show the known lifespans of the artists. Dotted lines show approximate lifespans. Names of artists are placed in the regions of their maximum production (not where they were born or trained). If artists were active in more than one region, the other region is shown in brackets. For example, under Rome, 'Raphael (& Florence)' means 'worked substantially in Florence as well as Rome.' D=Dutch, Fl=Flemish.

BEYOND THE ALPS

THE LOW COUNTRIES

Broederlam (Fl) — Petrus C
Jan van Eyck (Fl)
Roger van der Weyden (Fl)
Dirck Bouts (D)
Limbourg brothers *(& France)*
Sluter *(& France)*
Campin (Fl)

GERMANY

Konrad Witz *(& Basle)*
Multscher
Stephan Lochner
Mart
Lukas Moser

FRANCE

Fouquet

SPAIN

Andrea del Sarto

Ghirlandaio

Cellini *(& Rome & Paris)*

Leonardo da Vinci *(& Milan)*

Lorenzo di Credi

Baccio Bandinelli

Andrea Sansovino

Albertinelli

Pontormo

Bronzino

nio Pollaiuolo

Piero Pollaiuolo

Fra Bartolommeo

Filippino Lippi

S. Sepolcro & Rome)

Rosso Fiorentino *(& Fontainebleau)*

Vasari

Michelangelo *(& Rome)*

Botticelli

Giovanni Bologna d. 1608

Pietro Torrigiano *(& England)*

Antonio da Sangallo the Younger

Signorelli *(& Florence)*

Bramante *(& Milan)*

Perugino

Peruzzi

Raphael *(& Florence)*

Polidoro da Caravaggio

Parmigianino *(& Parma)*

Vignola

Salviati *(& Florence)*

Jacopino del Conte d. 1598

Sebastiano Serlio

Palma Vecchio

Giovanni Bellini

Foppa

& Ferrara)

Primaticcio *(& Fontainebleau)*

Lorenzo Lotto

Mantegna

Palladio d. 1580

Alvise Vivarini

Bassano d. 1592

Pietro Lombardo

Tullio Lombardo

Antonio Lombardo

Tintoretto d. 1594

Cima da Conegliano

Alessandro Vittoria d. 1608

Carpaccio

Veronese d. 1588

Antico

Giorgione

Pordenone

Michele Sanmicheli

Sebastiano del Piombo *(& Rome)*

Jacopo Sansovino

Titian

Correggio

Giulio Romano

Leone Leoni d. 1590

Patenir (Fl)

Memlinc (Fl)

Pieter Breughel the Elder (Fl)

Jan van Scorel (D)

Maerten van Heemskerck (D)

Spranger (Fl) d. 1611

Mabuse (Fl)

Adriaen de Vries d. 1626

Hugo van der Goes (Fl)

Bosch (D)

Quentin Massys (Fl)

Gerard David (Fl)

Geertgen tot Sint Jans (D)

Veit Stoss

Dürer

Riemenschneider

Altdorfer

chael Pacher

er

Adam Krafft

Grünewald

Lukas Cranach the Elder

Hermann Vischer the Younger

Hans Holbein the Younger *(& Basle & England)*

Jamnitzer d. 1585

Jean Clouet

Philibert de l'Orme

Lescot

Germain Pilon d. 1590

Goujon

Pedro Machuca

Berruguete

Juan Bautista de Toledo

Herrera d. 1597

El Greco d. 1614

Biographical Notes on Artists

AGOSTINO di Duccio. Florentine sculptor; b. 1418; worked both in Florence and outside at Modena, Rimini, Perugia and Bologna; d. 1481.

ALBERTI, Leone Battista. Florentine scholar and architect; b. probably 1404 at Genoa; 1428 returned to Florence but then entered papal civil service and travelled widely; main architectural works at Florence, Rimini and Mantua; d. 1472.

ALBERTINELLI, Mariotto. Florentine painter; b. 1474; lived and worked in Florence; d. 1515.

ALTDORFER, Albrecht. Bavarian painter, draughtsman and etcher; b. c. 1480; worked mainly at Regensburg (Ratisbon). A leading artist of the Danube School; d. 1538.

ANGELICO, Fra. Florentine painter; probably b. c. 1400; entered Dominican convent at Fiesole, near Florence; worked mainly in Florence but visited Rome c. 1446–9; revisited Rome where d. 1455.

ANTICO (properly Piero Jacopo Alari Bonacolsi). Mantuan bronze sculptor; b. probably c. 1460; worked at Gonzaga court in Mantua but visited Rome 1497; d. 1528.

ANTONELLO da Messina. Sicilian painter; b. c. 1430; worked at Naples and Messina but visited Venice 1475–6; d. at Messina 1479.

BANDINELLI, Baccio. Florentine sculptor, goldsmith and painter; b. 1493; although visited Rome c. 1536–41, worked mainly in Florence where d. 1560.

BARBARI, Jacopo de'. Venetian painter and engraver; b. c. 1445; worked first in Venice and after 1500 in Germany and Netherlands; d. c. 1516.

BARTOLOMMEO, Fra (properly Bartolommeo della Porta). Florentine painter; b. c. 1474; entered Dominican convent of S. Marco in Florence, 1500; worked mainly in Florence but visited Venice in 1508 and Rome c. 1514; d. c. 1517.

BASSANO (properly Jacopo da Ponte). Venetian painter; b. c. 1515; trained in Venice but worked entirely at Bassano; d. 1592.

BELLECHOSE, Henri. Flemish painter; active by 1415 when appointed court painter to Duke of Burgundy in Dijon; d. there 1440–4.

BELLINI, Giovanni. Venetian painter; b. c. 1430, son of Jacopo Bellini; worked almost exclusively in Venice where d. 1516.

BELLINI, Jacopo. Venetian painter; b. c. 1400; probably in Florence 1423 under Gentile da Fabriano, but worked mainly in Venice up to his death 1470–1.

BERRUGUETE, Alonso. Spanish sculptor, painter and architect; b. c. 1486; after c. 1504 in Italy (esp. Florence); by 1520 returned to Spain; worked especially at Valladolid and Toledo; d. at Toledo 1561.

BERTOLDO di Giovanni. Florentine sculptor; b. probably c. 1420; lived and worked in Florence where d. 1491.

BOLOGNA, Giovanni. Flemish sculptor; b. 1529 at Douai; trained in Flanders but moved to Italy c. 1554; worked mainly in Florence apart from one major commission in Bologna (1563–7); d. 1608.

BONIFAZIO de' Pitati. Venetian painter; b. 1487; lived and worked in Venice; d. 1553.

BOSCH, Hieronymus. Dutch painter; b. c. 1450 probably at 's Hertogenbosch where lived and d. 1516.

BOTTICELLI, Sandro. Florentine painter; b. c. 1445; worked mainly in Florence although visited Rome 1481–2 to paint in Sistine chapel; alleged to have been much influenced by the preaching of Savonarola; d. 1510.

BOUTS, Dirck. Dutch painter b. c. 1415 at Haarlem; worked mainly at Louvain where d. 1475.

BRAMANTE, Donato. Architect from the Marches; b. 1444 near Urbino; 1477 in Bergamo; c. 1479–99 worked mainly in Milan and Pavia; 1499 moved to Rome where d. 1514.

BREUGHEL, Pieter. Flemish painter; b. 1525–30; worked mainly at Antwerp and Brussels; c. 1552–4 visited Italy including Rome and Sicily; d. 1569.

BROEDERLAM, Melchior. Flemish painter active from 1381; 1385 court painter to Philip the Bold, Duke of Burgundy; no further knowledge after 1409.

BRONZINO (properly Agnolo Allori). Florentine painter; b. 1503; worked mainly in Florence where became court painter to Duke Cosimo I de' Medici; d. 1572.

BRUNELLESCHI, Filippo. Florentine sculptor and architect; b. 1377; worked mainly in and near Florence but visited Rome probably c. 1405 and c. 1430–3; d. 1446.

CAMPIN, Robert. Flemish painter; b. 1378–9; worked mainly at Tournai; it seems likely that his work is that often given to the so-called Master of Flémalle. The identification is by no means certain but for the sake of simplicity it is accepted here without argument; d. 1444.

CARAVAGGIO, Polidoro da. Italian painter; b. probably during 1490s; active in Rome to 1528; thereafter active in Naples and Messina until d. 1543.

CARPACCIO, Vittore. Venetian painter; b. c. 1465; worked almost exclusively in Venice; d. 1523–6.

CASTAGNO, Andrea del. Florentine painter; b. probably 1423; 1442 visited Venice but worked mainly in Florence; d. 1457.

CELLINI, Benvenuto. Florentine sculptor and goldsmith; b. 1500; 1519–40 worked mainly in Rome with visits to Florence, Venice and France; 1540–5 stayed in France; from 1545 mainly in Florence where d. 1571.

CHRISTUS, Petrus. Flemish painter; b. c. 1420; after 1444 worked mainly in Bruges; d. 1472–3.

CIMA da Conegliano. Venetian painter; b. 1459–60; worked mainly in Venice; d. 1517–18.

CLOUET, Jean. Flemish painter; court painter to French king; active by 1509; d. 1540–1.

CONTE, Jacopino del. Florentine painter; b. 1510; 1538 moved to Rome where lived and worked; d. there 1598.

CORREGGIO, Antonio. Milanese painter; b. probably 1494; worked mainly in Correggio and Parma; d. 1534.

CRANACH, Lukas. German painter, etcher and designer of woodcuts; b. 1472; in Vienna 1503 but from 1505 worked almost entirely at Wittenberg where he became court painter to Elector of Saxony; d. 1553.

CREDI, Lorenzo di. Florentine painter; b. c. 1458; lived and worked in Florence; d. 1537.

DAVID, Gerard. Flemish painter; b. c. 1460 at Oudewater in Holland; by 1483 in Bruges; worked mainly in Bruges, except for visit to Antwerp 1515; d. at Bruges 1523.

DESIDERIO da Settignano. Florentine sculptor; b. 1428; worked in Florence where d. 1464.

DONATELLO. Florentine sculptor; b. 1386; trained and worked in Florence; 1431–3 visited Rome; returned to Florence until stay in Padua 1443–53; returned to Florence where d. 1466.

DÜRER, Albrecht. Franconian painter, engraver and designer of woodcuts, b. 1471 at Nürnberg where he made his home; visited Venice 1494–5 and again 1505–7; 1512 court painter to Maximilian I and subsequently to his son Charles V; visited the Netherlands 1520; d. 1528.

EYCK, Jan van. Flemish painter; active from 1422, first as court painter to John, Count of Holland; 1425 court painter to Philip the Good, Duke of Burgundy; from c. 1430 lived at Bruges until d. 1441.

FILARETE (properly Antonio di Pietro Averlino). Italian sculptor and architect; b. c. 1400 in Florence; probably moved to Rome c. 1433; returned to Florence 1447 and journeyed in N. Italy until summoned to Milan 1451; perhaps returned to Rome c. 1465; d. c. 1469.

FIORE, Jacobello del. Venetian painter; active by 1400; lived and worked mainly in Venice where d. 1439.

FOPPA, Vincenzo. Brescian painter; b. 1427–30; court painter to the Dukes of Milan; worked mainly in Milan and Pavia; several visits to Genoa; d. 1515–16.

FOUQUET, Jean. French painter; b. c. 1420 at Tours; visited Rome probably during 1440s but worked mainly for French court at Tours; court painter 1475; d. 1481 or before.

GEERTGEN tot Sint Jans. Dutch painter, said to have died c. 1490 aged 28; worked at Haarlem.

GENTILE da Fabriano. Painter from the Marches; b. c. 1370; 1408–9 worked in Doges' Palace, Venice; 1414–19 at Brescia; 1422–5 in Florence; 1425–6 in Siena; 1427 in Rome, where d. 1427.

GERHAERT, Nikolaus. Origins unknown; 1462–7 in Strasbourg; 1467 moved to Vienna; 1472 living in Wiener-Neustadt; probably d. by 1487.

GHIBERTI, Lorenzo. Florentine sculptor and goldsmith with some claims to be painter and architect as well; b. 1378; active mainly in Florence apart from work in Siena 1417–27 and trip to Venice 1424; d. 1455.

GHIRLANDAIO, Domenico. Florentine painter; b. 1449; worked mainly in Florence but visited Rome 1481–2 to paint in Sistine chapel; d. 1494.

GIORGIONE. Venetian painter; b. 1476–8; worked mainly in Venice; d. 1510.

GIUSTI, Antonio. Florentine sculptor; b. before 1485; by 1504 in France (Tours); lived and worked there until d. 1519.

GIUSTI, Giovanni. Florentine sculptor, younger brother of Antonio; b. 1485; by 1504 in France (Tours); lived and worked there until d. 1549.

GOES, Hugo van der. Flemish painter; b. c. 1445 probably at Ghent; lived at Ghent until c. 1475 when became lay brother of Augustinian house of Roode Clooster near Brussels; d. 1482.

GOSSAERT, Jan (MABUSE). Flemish painter; b. c. 1480; worked mainly in Antwerp; visited Italy 1508; d. c. 1533.

GOUJON, Jean. French sculptor and architect; b. perhaps *c.* 1510; active first in Rouen (1530s) and after *c.* 1540 mainly in Paris; d. after 1562.

GRASSER, Erasmus. Bavarian sculptor and architect; b. *c.* 1450; lived and worked mainly in and around Munich where d. 1526.

GRECO, El (properly Domenikos Theotocopoulos). Painter of Cretan origin; b. 1541; trained in Venice; *c.* 1570 moved to Rome and (by 1577) to Spain. Lived mainly in Toledo, where d. 1614.

GRÜNEWALD (properly Mathias Neithardt-Gothardt). Würzburg painter; b. *c.* 1475; by 1501 in Seligenstadt; lived and worked mainly in and near Seligenstadt; d. 1528.

HEEMSKERCK, Maerten van. Dutch painter; b. 1498; lived and worked mainly at Haarlem; visited Rome 1532–5; d. 1574.

HOLBEIN, Hans, the Younger. Bavarian painter; b. 1497–8 at Augsburg; by 1515 in Basle where he mainly lived until 1526 when moved to England; after further short stay at Basle, returned to England, where lived until d. 1543.

JAMNITZER, Wenzel. Austrian goldsmith; b. 1508 at Vienna; by 1534 a citizen of Nürnberg, where lived and d. 1585.

LEONARDO da Vinci. Florentine painter; b. 1452 at Vinci, near Florence; trained in Florence; *c.* 1482–99 in Milan; mainly in Florence 1500–6, serving under Cesare Borgia in the Romagna 1502–3; 1506–13 in Milan with visit to Florence 1507–8; 1513–17 in Rome; 1517 moved to France where d. 1519.

LEONI, Leone. Aretine sculptor; b. 1509; by 1537 in Padua; 1538–40 in Rome; 1542 began career as imperial sculptor and medallist in Milan with subsequent visits to Brussels and Augsburg; d. at Milan 1590.

LEONI, Pompeo. Son of Leone; b. *c.* 1533; until *c.* 1556 in Milan but thereafter lived mainly in Spain (Madrid) where d. 1608.

LESCOT, Pierre. French architect; b. 1500–15; worked mainly in Paris; d. 1578.

LIMBOURG, Pol, Hennequin and **Herman de.** Flemish painters and MS. illuminators; by 1400 in Paris; thence to court of Duke of Burgundy (1402) and Duke of Berry (*c.* 1409); all three d. before 1416.

LIPPI, Fra Filippo. Florentine painter; b. *c.* 1406; 1421 entered monastery of Sta Maria del Carmine; apart from visits to Padua (1434) and Spoleto (1466–9) worked mainly in or near Florence; d. 1469.

LIPPI, Filippino. Florentine painter, illegitimate son of Fra Filippo Lippi; b. 1457–8; worked mainly in Florence but visited and worked in Rome 1488–93; d. 1504.

LOMBARDO, Antonio. Lombard sculptor and architect; b. *c.* 1458; younger son of Pietro Lombardo; presumably worked in Venice *c.* 1474–1506; moved to Ferrara where d. 1516.

LOMBARDO, Pietro. Lombard sculptor and architect; b. perhaps 1435; 1464 in Padua; by 1474 in Venice where lived until d. 1515.

LOMBARDO, Tullio. Lombard sculptor and architect; b. *c.* 1455; elder son of Pietro Lombardo; lived and worked mainly in or near Venice presumably from *c.* 1474 until d. 1532.

LORENZO Monaco. Sienese painter; b. *c.* 1370–2; worked mainly in Florence where entered monastery of Sta Maria degli Angeli; d. *c.* 1422–5.

LOTTO, Lorenzo. Venetian painter; b. *c.* 1480; 1503–6 lived at Treviso; 1509 in Rome; 1513 in the Marches; 1513–26 lived and worked in Bergamo; 1526–42 mainly in Venice with visits to Bergamo and Marches; 1542–5 lived in Treviso; 1545–9 returned to Venice; 1549 departed for Marches where d. at Loreto 1556.

MACHUCA, Pedro. Spanish architect, sculptor and painter; first mention in Florence 1516; 1520 returned to Spain (Granada) where d. 1550.

MALOUEL, Jean. Flemish painter; by 1396 in Paris; 1397 court painter to Duke of Burgundy at Dijon; d. in Paris 1419.

MANTEGNA, Andrea. Paduan painter; b. *c.* 1431; 1453 married into Bellini family; worked in Padua up to *c.* 1460; thence moved to court of Mantua; visited Rome 1490 and worked in Vatican; apart from this lived and worked in and around Mantua until d. 1506.

MASACCIO. Florentine painter; b. 1401; worked in Florence and Pisa; went to Rome where d. *c.* 1428.

MASOLINO. Florentine painter; b. *c.* 1383–4; probably worked in Florence until *c.* 1430 except for visit to Hungary (1427); *c.* 1430 moved to Rome and thence (1435) to Castiglione d'Olona, near Milan. No further information, but d. probably 1440–7.

MASSYS, Quentin. Flemish painter; b. 1464–5 at Louvain; by 1491 moved to Antwerp where he lived for rest of life, apart from possible visit to Italy *c.* 1515; d. 1530.

MEMLINC, Hans. Flemish painter; b. perhaps *c.* 1445; lived and worked at Bruges where d. 1494.

MICHELANGELO. Florentine painter, sculptor and architect; b. 1475; trained in Florence where lived until 1505 apart from stay in Bologna and Rome 1495–1501; 1505–16 worked in Rome; 1516–34 in Florence; 1534 returned to Rome where d. 1564.

MICHELOZZO Michelozzi. Florentine sculptor, bronze-founder and architect; b. 1396; worked mainly in Florence but probably visited Milan *c.* 1460; d. 1472.

MOSER, Lukas. Painter from Weilderstadt; known only from Tiefenbronn altarpiece, 1431.

MULTSCHER, Hans. Swabian painter and sculptor; b. *c.* 1400; worked chiefly in or near Ulm; d. before 1467.

NANNI di Banco. Florentine sculptor; b. *c.* 1384; lived and worked in Florence where d. 1421.

ORLEY, Bernard van. Flemish painter; b. *c.* 1488; probably visited Italy but worked mainly in Brussels where d. 1541.

ORME, Philibert de l'. French architect; b. *c.* 1510; visited Rome *c.* 1533; *c.* 1540 went to Paris; worked mainly for French court until d. 1570.

PACHER, Michael. Tyrolean painter and sculptor; b. *c.* 1435; by 1462–3 in Brunico where lived and worked; d. there 1498.

PALLADIO, Andrea. Vicentine architect; b. 1508; lived and worked mainly in and around Vicenza; journeys to Rome 1540–1, 1544, 1546 and 1550; some important works in Venice; d. at Vicenza 1580.

PALMA Vecchio, Jacopo. Venetian painter; b. 1480; worked mainly in Venice where d. 1528.

PARMIGIANINO, Francesco. Milanese painter; b. 1503; worked in Parma until 1523 when moved to Rome. After Sack of Rome (1527) escaped north, finally (1530) returning to Parma where d. 1540.

PATENIR, Joachim. Flemish painter; worked probably mainly at Antwerp; d. *c.* 1524.

PERUGINO, Pietro. Perugian painter; b. *c.* 1445–50; trained partly in Umbria and partly in Florence; 1481–2 in Rome (Sistine chapel); worked thereafter mainly in Perugia with frequent visits elsewhere (Florence, Venice, Rome); d. 1523.

PERUZZI, Baldassare Tommaso. Sienese architect and painter; b. 1481; from 1503 lived and worked mainly in Rome apart from work in Bologna (1521–3) and a short return to Siena (1527–9); d. in Rome 1536.

PIERO della Francesca. Umbrian painter; b. *c.* 1410–20; trained in Florence; thereafter (1442) lived mainly at home in Borgo S. Sepolcro working at Ferrara (*c.* 1445), Rimini (1451), Arezzo (from *c.* 1452) and Rome (1459). In his later years, after 1478, he seems to have given up painting for theory; d. 1492.

PILON, Germain. French sculptor; b. *c.* 1530; by 1558 working for French court mainly in Paris; d. 1590.

PISANELLO, Antonio. Pisan painter and medallist who was trained and worked almost entirely in N. Italy; b. *c.* 1395; trained probably in Verona; *c.* 1415–22 in Venice; but *c.* 1431–2 in Rome; and *c.* 1448–9 probably in Naples; d. perhaps *c.* 1455.

PLEYDENWURFF, Hans. Probably Franconian painter; 1451 already active in Nürnberg where lived and worked; possible journeys to Cracow and Breslau; d. 1472.

POLLAIUOLO, Antonio. Florentine painter and sculptor; b. *c.* 1432; worked mainly in Florence until 1484 when moved to Rome where d. 1498.

POLLAIUOLO, Piero. Florentine painter; b. 1443; younger brother of Antonio; active in Florence until 1484 when moved with brother to Rome; d. there 1496.

PONTORMO, Jacopo. Florentine painter; b. 1494; lived and worked almost entirely in or near Florence where d. 1556.

PORDENONE, Giovanni Antonio. Friulian painter; b. *c.* 1483–4; worked mainly in or near Venice; commissions at Piacenza *c.* 1530 and Ferrara 1538; d. 1539.

PRIMATICCIO, Francesco. Bolognese painter, sculptor and architect; b. *c.* 1504–5; trained at Mantua; 1532 moved to French court at Fontainebleau; visited Rome 1540–2 and again 1546; 1563 revisited Bologna; d. 1570.

QUERCIA, Jacopo della. Sienese sculptor; b. *c.* 1374–5; *c.* 1406–25 worked mainly at Lucca and Siena; *c.* 1425 onwards divided attention between Siena and Bologna; d. 1438.

RAPHAEL. Painter and architect from the Marches; b. 1483; trained in Perugia, thence moved to Florence; *c.* 1508 moved to Rome, where d. 1520.

RIEMENSCHNEIDER, Tilman. Franconian sculptor; b. *c.* 1460; lived and worked in or near Würzburg; d. 1531.

ROBBIA, Luca della. Florentine sculptor; b. 1400; lived and worked mainly in and around Florence; d. 1482.

ROMANO, Giulio. Roman painter and architect; b. 1492 or 1499; worked in Rome until 1524 when moved to Mantua to work for Gonzaga family; d. 1546.

ROSSELLINO, Antonio. Florentine sculptor; b. 1427; worked mainly in and around Florence; d. c. 1479.

ROSSO Fiorentino, Giovanni Battista. Florentine painter; b. 1495; trained in Florence; 1523-7 in Rome; thence to Venice and France (1530); worked mainly at Fontainebleau; d. 1540.

SALVIATI, Francesco. Florentine painter; b. 1510; active in Florence until c. 1530; moved to Rome where lived and worked apart from journeys to Venice and north (1539–41), Florence (1544-8) and France (1554–5); d. in Rome 1563.

SANGALLO, Antonio da, the Younger. Florentine architect; b. 1483; 1503 moved to Rome; lived and worked almost entirely in and around Rome; d. 1546.

SANMICHELI, Michele. Veronese architect; b. 1484; c. 1500 moved to Rome where worked until 1527; thence entered service of Venetian state (1528) and worked mainly in Venice and Venetian provinces (esp. Verona); d. in Verona 1559.

SANSOVINO, Andrea. Florentine sculptor and architect; b. c. 1460; visits to Portugal in 1490s; moved to Rome 1505 and thence as official architect to Loreto; d. 1529.

SANSOVINO, Jacopo. Florentine sculptor; b. 1486; worked in Florence and Rome up to 1527 when moved to Venice; d. there 1570.

SARTO, Andrea del. Florentine painter; b. 1486; worked mainly in and near Florence although visited France 1518–19; d. 1531.

SCHONGAUER, Martin. Alsatian painter and engraver; b. c. 1430; lived and worked mainly in or near Colmar; d. 1491 at Breisach.

SCOREL, Jan van. Dutch painter; b. 1495; trained in Amsterdam; by 1517 in Utrecht where lived and worked apart from journeys to Jerusalem (1520-4 via Carinthia and Venice, with stay in Rome) and France (1540); d. 1562.

SEBASTIANO del Piombo. Venetian painter; b. c. 1485; worked in Venice until 1511; moved to Rome where lived and worked until d. 1547.

SERLIO, Sebastiano. Bolognese painter and architect; b. 1475; 1514-27 lived and worked in Rome; thence moved to Venice and finally (1541) to France; d. in France 1554.

SIGNORELLI, Luca. Umbrian painter; b. 1441–50; c. 1475 probably visited Florence; 1482 in Rome (Sistine chapel); worked mainly in and around home town of Cortona; 1499–1503/4 at Orvieto; c. 1508 and 1513 again in Rome; d. 1523.

SLUTER, Claus. Dutch sculptor; origins uncertain; active c. 1380 onwards as sculptor of Philip the Bold, Duke of Burgundy, at Dijon; d. there 1406.

SPRANGER, Bartholomäus. Flemish painter and engraver; b. 1546 at Antwerp; 1565 moved to Paris and thence via Milan and Parma to Rome (1566); 1575–6 entered imperial service and moved to Vienna; d. in Prague 1611.

SQUARCIONE, Francesco. Paduan painter; b. 1397; worked mainly in and around Padua; d. 1468.

STOSS, Veit. Sculptor, painter and engraver, probably from Franconia; b. c. 1440; 1477 in Poland (Cracow) where lived mainly until 1496; thereafter lived and worked chiefly in region of Nürnberg; d. 1533.

TINTORETTO, Jacopo. Venetian painter; b. 1518; lived and worked mainly in Venice where d. 1594.

TITIAN. Venetian painter; b. c. 1490; lived and worked almost entirely in and around Venice apart from a visit to Rome (1545–6) and visits to Augsburg (1548–9 and 1550–1); d. 1576.

TOLEDO, Juan Bautista de. Spanish architect; trained in Rome; active in Naples 1540s; before July 1559 returned to Spain; d. 1567.

TORRIGIANO, Pietro. Florentine sculptor; b. 1472; trained in Florence but worked mainly in England (1511–18) and Spain where d. 1528.

TURA, Cosmè. Ferrarese painter; b. before 1431; from 1451 court painter at Ferrara until 1486; d. 1495.

UCCELLO, Paolo. Florentine painter; b. 1396-7; lived and worked mainly in Florence but visited Venice (1425) and probably Urbino (c. 1465-9); d. 1475.

VAGA, Pierino del. Florentine painter; b. 1501; active mainly in Rome until 1527; thence moved to Genoa; worked in Genoa and Pisa until 1539; returned to Rome where d. 1547.

VASARI, Giorgio. Aretine painter and writer; b. 1511; trained in Florence; worked mainly in Florence, Rome and Arezzo; author of *The Lives of the Most Excellent Italian Architects, Painters and Sculptors*, first edition 1550, second enlarged edition 1568; d. 1574.

VENEZIANO, Domenico. Perhaps Venetian painter but trained in Florence; b. probably c. 1410; worked in Florence; d. 1461.

VERONESE, Paolo. Veronese painter; b. 1528; lived and worked in Venice and the Veneto; d. 1588.

VERROCCHIO, Andrea del. Florentine painter, sculptor and goldsmith; b. c. 1435; worked mainly in Florence but from c. 1479 was frequently in Venice where d. 1488.

VIGNOLA, Giacomo Barozzi da. Italian architect; b. 1507; trained in Bologna; c. 1530 moved to Rome; 1541 visited France; 1546 worked for Farnese family in Parma; thereafter worked within and outside Rome for Farnese family and on other commissions; d. 1573.

VITTORIA, Alessandro. Venetian sculptor; b. 1525; lived and worked in Venice where d. 1608.

VIVARINI, Alvise. Venetian painter; son of Antonio; active from 1457; d. 1503–5.

VIVARINI, Antonio. Venetian painter; active from c. 1440; d. 1476–84.

VIVARINI, Bartolommeo. Venetian painter; brother of Antonio; active from c. 1450; d. 1499.

VRIES, Adriaen de. Dutch sculptor; b. c. 1560 at The Hague; trained in Florence; by c. 1590 in Rome; 1596–1601 active in Augsburg; thence to Prague where mainly lived and worked until d. 1626.

WEYDEN, Roger van der. Flemish painter; b. c. 1399-1400; trained in Tournai; by 1436 in Brussels, where lived and worked; perhaps visited Beaune (Burgundy) c. 1446 and Rome 1450; d. 1464.

WITZ, Conrad. German painter; b. c. 1400-10; 1434 already at Basle, Switzerland, where lived and worked; d. 1444-6.

Index

The numbers in heavy type refer to colour plates; italic numbers refer to black and white illustrations.

Acknowledgements

Photographs were provided by the following:

Colour: A.C.L., Brussels 18; Emil Bauer, Nürnberg 67, 75; Bibliothèque Nationale, Paris 11; J. Blauel, Munich 65, 79; Bowes Museum, Barnard Castle, Durham 72; Cine Brunel and Co., Lugano 70; A. C. Cooper, London 33, 98; Bruno Del Priore, Rome 47; Giraudon, Paris 1, 12, 14, 20, 69, 86, 91; Paul Hamlyn Archive 35; Hessisches Landesmuseum, Darmstadt 80; Michael Holford, London 6, 17, 30, 34, 36, 48, 49, 51, 52, 62, 68, 71, 77, 90, 95; Jaqueline Hyde, Paris 13; Lossen-Foto, Heidelberg 78; Metropolitan Museum of Art, New York 15; E. Meyer, Vienna 64, 66, 73, 74, 76, 87; National Gallery of Art, Washington 21; Photo Precision, St Albans 81; Rupert Roddam, Glasgow 89; Scala, Florence 2, 3, 4, 5, 7, 8, 9, 10, 19, 22, 24, 25, 26, 27, 28, 29, 31, 32, 38, 39, 40, 41, 42, 44, 45, 46, 53, 54, 56, 57, 59, 60, 61, 63, 82, 83, 84, 85, 88, 93, 94, 96, 97, 99, 100, and back cover; State Museums, Berlin-Dahlem 37, 43; Vasari, Rome 23, 50, 55, 58, 92; J. Ziolo, Paris 16

Black and White: Accademia, Venice 91; A.C.L., Brussels 66; Alinari, Florence 1, 4, 5, 6, 7, 8, 9, 10, 11, 12, 13, 15, 25, 28, 31, 36, 37, 40, 43, 44, 45, 86, 95, 101, 102, 103, 104; Alinari/Anderson, Florence 27, 38, 39, 52, 53, 57, 61, 87, 93, 99; Anderson/Giraudon, Paris 2, 24; Archives Photographiques, Paris 79; Bavaria Verlag 78; Bayerische Staatsgemäldesammlungen, Munich 51; Bildarchiv Foto Marburg 3, 19, 20, 69, 70, 71, 72, 73, 74; E. Boudot-Lamotte, Paris 41; British Museum, London 23, 32, 47, 77; Brogi, Florence 14, 26, 29; Bulloz, Paris 22; Courtauld Institute, London 48, 81; Foto Feruzzi, Venice 89, 100; Foto Fisa, Barcelona 83; John Freeman, London 55, 94; Gabinetto Fotografico Nazionale, Rome 59, 60; Giraudon, Paris 21, 46, 49, 50, 65, 75, 80, 82, 90; Hills and Saunders, Eton 68; Michael Holford, London 64; Larousse, Paris 42, 56, 63; Mansell/Alinari, London 34; Mansell/Anderson, London 35; Mansell/Brogi, London 30; MAS, Barcelona 84, 85; Metropolitan Museum of Art, New York 88; Museu Nacional de Arte Antiga, Lisbon 67; National Gallery, London 62; National Gallery, Prague 17, 18; Rheinisches Bildarchiv, Cologne 33; Foto Rossi, Venice 92; Oscar Savio, Rome 54; Scala, Florence 98; Toni Schneiders/Bavaria Verlag 76; Soprintendenza alle Gallerie, Florence 16; Städelsches Kunstinstitut, Frankfurt 96; Victoria and Albert Museum, London 97; Wallace Collection, London 58

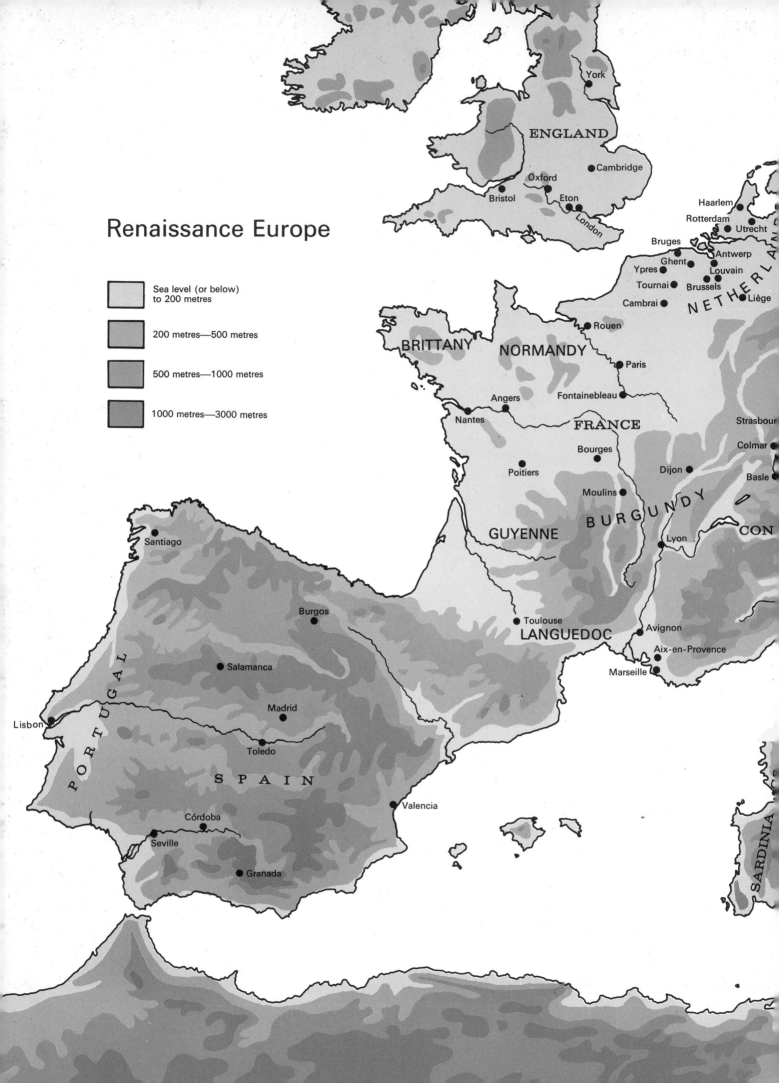

Renaissance Europe

Sea level (or below)
to 200 metres

200 metres—500 metres

500 metres—1000 metres

1000 metres—3000 metres

York

ENGLAND

Cambridge

Oxford
Bristol
Eton
London

Haarlem
Rotterdam
Utrecht
Bruges
Antwerp
Ypres   Ghent   Louvain
Tournai   Brussels
Cambrai   NETHERLAND   Liège

Rouen

BRITTANY   NORMANDY

Paris

Angers   Fontainebleau
Nantes   FRANCE

Strasbour

Bourges   Colmar

Poitiers   Dijon   Basle

Moulins   BURGUNDY   CON

Santiago   GUYENNE

Lyon

Toulouse   Avignon
LANGUEDOC   Aix-en-Provence
Marseille

Burgos

Salamanca

Madrid

Lisbon   PORTUGAL

Toledo

SPAIN

Córdoba   Valencia

Seville

Granada

SARDINIA